G000097398

SACRED
PRESENCE

as
the
Awareness

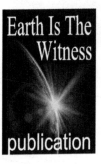

SACRED PRESENCE

as

the

Awareness

Petar Umiljanovic

Copyright © 2023 by Petar Umiljanovic

All rights reserved.

No part of this publication may be reproduced, distributed, or
transmitted in any form or by any means, including photocopying,
recording, or other electronic or mechanical methods, without the
prior written permission of the publisher, except in the case of
brief quotations embodied in critical reviews and certain
other non-commercial uses permitted by copyright law.

For permission requests, write to the author.

Earth Is The Witness publication

ISBN 9798863791586

Cover design by
Petar Umiljanovic

Earth Is The Witness

This is my Intellect
my Heart & Soul

speaking to You
in words of
Infinite Consciousness

my endless Love
for this World

for You

As You read it through

it will reward You
being forever written in
the Universe's Book of Life

I LOVE YOU

Contents

*I dedicate this book to You, Dear Reader,
for having the courage to follow your sense
of waking awareness, tracing her back to
the one source of pure consciousness*

INTRODUCTION

Welcome, Dear Reader!

You and I shall once again dive deep into the nature of consciousness, this time with a specific focus on the Presence as the Awareness, which is indeed so sacred to us that it deserves closer, more intimate introspection.

The most universal spiritual feeling is the sense of something bigger and greater out there. Some people call this sense God, whereas countless others don't believe in God, rather, they simply remain with the initial more basic sense. And this is the correct attitude to have.

To ensure that I describe this phenomenon with absolute precision, aiming to inspire the true spiritual awakening associated with these universal and personal truths, I will refer to this sense as Sacred Presence.

In our previous books, we have already explored how Consciousness is the essential mystery and solution pertinent to existence. Here we will continue to extrapolate on that same essence with even deeper, far-reaching inner and outer observations of consciousness.

We will strike at the heart of many dilemmas, consider some common causes and unconscious traits that explain why people tend to have such problems, then offer clear-cut, straight-to-the-point advice on how to identify such traits and, in turn, how to regain our natural sense of being aware.

One needs to be careful, though, when dealing with so many types of words & terms that are, on the one hand describing similar experiences & problems, and on the other, offer teachings & inspiration.

For this reason, we will look at the several flavours of consciousness to see where they will lead us and learn to differentiate between them before returning to the most familiar to us, our own point of Awareness.

You are most welcome to open your heart and experience
the uneasy depth, as well as the natural,
healing surface of your being.

Chapter 1

$\mathcal{P}$RESENCE

PRESENT

What is Present? What do we mean by the Present? Is it the now, today, or what is happening at the current moment? Is it what is perceived at the moment, in this moment, which is the only time or space the now can be in? 'Be in the now, be present', might sound like an overused statement today. But it is at the core of life, of self-awareness, of being self-aware.

We know of the present because of the things we can notice through our immediate awareness.

And we can only be aware now, in the present moment, of the present moment. But that rarely happens. We are mostly aware of what arises in the present, such as thoughts and emotions. We can also be aware of thoughts about the past or future, and this of course happens in the now, in the present.

The present is all tHere ever is.

There are no actual moments, only a constant nowness. We can easily conclude that everything is happening now. Every experience of perceptions, sensations, feelings, and thoughts, is known only in the present. And is only known by one's own awareness.

What notice and knows in the present,
is awareness of whatever is noticed.

Even our identity, our sense of ourselves as a person, is being aware by awareness. We are not a person, which is a collection of ideas, thoughts, and beliefs. We are nothing that we can be aware of. Hence, when awareness settles, the only thing that remains is consciousness. We are the awareness of something, or, more precisely, we are the awareness itself when engaged by perception. But in its undisturbed unengaged state, we are consciousness.

Make the present full of your presence.

Consciousness is present. These two concepts are identical. Nothing exists outside consciousness, and nothing happens outside the present. That isness is the true fundamental state of existence.

Present, isness, beingness, consciousness.

THOUGHT

How we experience life comes down to our personal relationship with our thoughts, but primarily with the identified resulting consequences of belief and emotion.

A thought appears in the present, but a thought takes us out of our awareness and directs it to itself; it grabs our attention and we end up missing out on the present by being lost in thought. And thoughts appear suddenly, unforeseen, at random, and we don't choose them, otherwise, we would know them in advance, or we would have to think them before they appear. They just arise in our awareness, in the mind (although there is no such thing as the mind, just a perceiver's state of remembrance). What we call the mind is essentially a bundle of memories from which we seem to access thoughts, one at a time.

A thought is a notification sent to the awareness informing it that it is losing consciousness. Every open notification and every thought experienced takes you away from the present, as you start to believe and identify with your thoughts, thus creating emotions, leading to the point of forgetting your conscious essence.

Emotion is felt proof that we have identified with the story. But thoughts themselves are not good or bad, they don't carry a sign positive or negative, they are merely flashes in consciousness, and our job is to refrain from giving any attention to those flashes and to leave the notifications unopened.

Most people have completely identified with the whole story and thought narrative in their minds that there is no separation between the two, they are their mind, their emotions, their reactions. They say what they think, and they say it directly and immediately. They have already expressed it before they have even thought of it.

With such instant identification with themselves, most human conversation consists of habitual, self-centred, emotional and social comfort, with no other meaning than to repeat, state, and claim one's state of mind that also fulfils the need to acknowledge the presence of others. Confirming and establishing one's own presence makes one feel better about speaking,

not to mention how it evades the silence that is so
unbearably uncomfortable for them.

In short, we speak primarily for the sake of speaking,
to satisfy the habit of speaking, but not to convey or
contribute any real meaning to life or the present
moment.

And don't get me wrong, the world has exploded
with original thought, wisdom, and the opening up
of awareness. So many are waking up from the dream
of themselves and the world. So many are priceless
contributions to a state of beingness.

But where do you think you belong in that arena
of "*Great minds discuss ideas; average minds discuss events;
small minds discuss people?*" Have you yourself enquired
into the nature of the one who speaks? Have you re-
examined all the little ticks and urges that prompt you
to act? Are you able to observe the voice in your head,
the speaker, the listener? Do you know the one who
thinks and the one who thinks that it thinks?
If we are the ones who think, why would we
think absolute nonsense most of the time?

It certainly seems that thinking is an involuntary
occurrence in awareness. We are awareness aware of
these internal and external processes. But if the awareness is aware, what is aware of awareness' awareness?
How many thinkers and how many awareness' seem
to be there? How many personalities are here?

*THere can only be one unwavering awareness
that we call pure consciousness.*

All other subsequent dialogues and self-awareness'
are dilutions of that conscious fundamental platform
of experience.

To notice and know, to examine all these facets of the
self we must attend to our pure consciousness. Only by
abiding as the awareness, obviously in the present, can
we explore the true nature of consciousness and all the
subsequent appearances such as the mind, thoughts and
feelings. This is done by focus, attention, observation,
meditation, contemplation, noticing, realising,
understanding, comprehending, as well as by
being fully honest with ourselves while being aware.

Now, to distinguish the present from the appearances
within it, from sense perceptions, from the awareness of
sense itself, we will examine the sense of presence.

THE SENSE OF GOD

Humans are generally the same species, anywhere
in the world, with the same perceptions, sensations and

feelings. They all sense something bigger than themselves, which we call God in the West, Tao in the East and
Spirit anywhere else. That sensation is the sacred
presence, and it is felt through our point of awareness.

*Without us, there would just be oneness, the unison
of duality, the constancy of consciousness.*

What I am suggesting is that the ultimate sense we
feel as God can only be our awareness, because after
quieting our mind, it is the only sense there is.

Countless people throughout history report seeing,
feeling and meeting angels, demons, aliens, ghosts,
fairies, God and all types of beings. I'm not denying their
sensory experience, I do think there are entities out there
in some shape and form, but we will not go into it here.
My purpose is not to discourage any such encounters,
or belief in God, as every instance in life has a broader
significance. But my goal is to look deeper and point
to the obvious natural consciousness as the answer
to most of our beliefs, desires and problems.

Our goal is to be as real and true as we possibly can,
to reexamine our day-to-day perceptions and become
serious about the significance of our senses. We have to
be absolutely honest with ourselves, come back to our
senses and regain natural awareness back from the mind.

To do that, we have to relax in our innermost being, letting go of any and every belief.

So, it is not that God doesn't exist, because what we think and feel to be God is truly here. But it is about correctly recognising the real origin of such perceptions and putting them into a proper place of understanding.

God as the one universal knowing is actually all that exists,
the one consciousness, and we, as separate beings,
are but thoughts in his mind.

Being in the present is God's plan, while following thought and identity is a temporary fate of the universe. By eating from the tree of fear, shame and ignorance, we have strayed away from God's pure presence, from the blissful garden of infinite consciousness.

Be present, be in the now, and feel God's being directly as your own beingness. Abide in that sacred space by remaining aware and conscious, dedicate your intention to it, and practice peace by being peaceful.

We feel other people's presence when we see them, but sometimes we feel the invisible presence that we can not explain. I'm not talking about the sense that somebody is looking at us from behind, but about the real invisible presence, of the ghostly or spiritual type.

And sure there could be spirits, poltergeists, entities, angels and demons, but none of these explain the one presence that underlies all others. We have given that presence a name – God – however, we could describe this presence as more of a primordial sense of being, which is consciousness, inherently known when met by our awareness.

We cherish photos of loved ones and statues of historic people because the presence of the one we wish to remember is felt there in these physical reminders. We keep pets too as feeling their presence alleviates our loneliness.

But the biggest presence we feel is the closeness of another human being. So we know how it feels when someone or something is present – we feel it. Likewise, the feeling of God is legitimate and the most common type of invisible presence. And this presence is absolutely real. In fact, this presence is the only true presence because it constitutes the one consciousness itself.

The person who feels this presence is the illusory sense here. God, that is consciousness, is the one and only single undeniable presence that is. Yes, this means that You and I are not real. We are but imagination in

God's mind. He is literally dreaming us into reality. There is no other answer, no other option, and no other conclusion once we surrender to the intelligence of consciousness. We should stop asking whether God exists. Instead, we ought to enquire into our own validity as aware beings and see what remains. Any sincere scrutiny of this nature will lead to one answer, that we are solely consciousness – an awareness behind which we can not hide.

> *It takes an honest awareness to*
> *realise itself as consciousness.*

What people refer to as God, is simply their own presence as the awareness. And God is literally that, he is the oneness of consciousness, the feeling of unconditional love, which is exactly what people are describing. We have substituted our most natural and intimate self for the idea of an outside influence that we believe is a sense of God.

> *The presence that we feel is our own higher-self awareness.*

People report this ultimate presence in near-death experiences, describing an utmost feeling of home, unconditional love and the knowing that everything is alright. This experience is deepened because we don't feel the body at that moment, but only our presence, which is finally free and limitless. This is the feeling of heavenly bliss, but it is more of a state than a feeling. It is our soul's true nature, one available to us always, for which reason many of those who return to the body hold on to that sense of secure light, love and peace throughout their life.

Presence can be felt as sensing something or someone outside of ourselves, or as the pure presence of beingness, which is inseparable from who we are as awareness, and it is not felt or experienced but, rather, known as consciousness that we are.

We feel God as all present, all-knowing, always with us and projected as an all-loving heavenly father. This correlates with presence as awareness, which is always here and is the space where everything in our lives happens. In fact, it is life, existence and beingness.

But to spiritually make sense of this divine sensation, we have mislabelled our own present being as God's presence. We have separated *the oneness* and we are experiencing duality, so we end up praying, begging, looking for God, or cursing, running and hiding from him. All the while our awareness – the true free sacred presence – is present throughout the ordeal.

Again, people's professed experience of God would simply be their own higher self, their true self and their soul when freed of mind. Hence, the voices in their head are merely their own heart talk and channelled wisdom. This is all knowledge that the soul naturally possesses and abides in when it is stripped of the mind's limitations and fear.

This knowledge is universal, but it can come with a distinctive voice and specific flavour of teaching, reflected in the written Bibles and wisdom traditions throughout history. But mortal men have been trying to interpret its meaning, tampering with the original teaching in doing so. As such, there is much confusion in the texts and translations.

Now, given all the reports about angels, souls, ghosts, spirits and of deceased contacting their loved ones, there is no doubt that many souls do interact with humanity, but, in most cases, we don't have to look further than our own guiding soul, which is always present, it is us, and we are a dream in our soul's imagination of ourselves.

When you die, you will extend your vision across the universe and forget about the Earth fast. it will seem like a dream, like a glitch in the matrix of universal experience. For this reason, most souls don't come back to Earth. After a split second of seeing and feeling the infinite freedom of spiritual existence, they are gone forever.

The reason the Earth feels familiar, as though we have

been here before, is attributable to past lives memories in some cases, but, for the most part, it is because we don't remember anything else. We confuse the familiar feeling of presence (which is always our actual and current experience) with the sense that this situation has already happened, irrespective of the experience.

Such confusion happens because of the complex stories that our minds create to interpret life's plethora of rich perceptual experiences. This is when we need to identify the main catalyst of confusion that results in, all the subsequent experiences that inevitably follow. This scenario remains unchanged throughout history.

Humans are born, they start to explore the world, they learn about themselves as separate beings, they develop their sense of identity and eventually manifest a complex world of education, laws, nations, traditions, countless stories and destinies.

SPIRITUALITY

The higher self is one's true self when stripped of fear. It is our pure soul, in most cases speaking through our open heart, hence the term 'heart talk'.

> *This higher self, or conscious self is a knower of*
> *true knowledge and a sage of true wisdom.*

You could be practising spirituality your entire life and never meet your higher self, or you could have a first meditation and fully channel your higher self. There is no pre-requisite for the awakening of your higher self, and it is similar to awakening itself. But one doesn't imply the other. We can compare one's higher self to the concept of 'the descending of the Holy Ghost unto you'. It is the sacred presence, the knowing of being, without any end.

If you want to know the universal knowledge, then you must align yourself to that perception, to pure consciousness. Likewise, if you want to be in God's mercy, you be the mercy. You don't ask or receive a blessing, you are the blessing. Don't wait or seek holiness, abundance or enlightenment. Drop the idea of not being it already, and realise your true worthiness in every moment by staying present. Then, God's sacred presence will shine as the light of your awareness.

Priests, monks, clergy, and other religious folks talk about feeling the call to God. What they are really feeling is freedom from themselves. Their belief they are rebirthing in the endless feeling of God's love is, in fact, the feeling of freedom in infinite consciousness. Their perception are partially obscured by religious beliefs.

Humanity has been stuck in the egoic sense of consciousness for ages, where every instance and glimpse of freedom from it has been unknowingly attributed to religion, to spirituality, to God. This has even been integrated into laws, rituals and commandments that believers are obligated to follow and obey in order to reach that holy salvation from self.

But spirituality can't be talking about your negative side, it only encourages your positives. It is not about pleasing some entities outside of yourself, such as God, saints, angels, or gurus, but is the ability to relax into your inner peace. It has nothing to do with doing but existing with a pure being. You don't force your way to God, you don't 'fake it until you make it'. You abide by awareness and benefit of the present peaceful experience.

There is no visible proof of God, but many cultures and faiths claim his existence on the base of faith and associated experiences. These are as varied and diverse as the individuals who feel them. But when we observe what is common among everybody, it is always and only our awareness and consciousness, which is God as the sacred presence.

Sacred Presence is God. It is what we feel as Spirit. We could call it God's love, which would be our pure consciousness. When we perceive the world with clear senses and empty minds, we experience unconditional love. That is God, Consciousness, the Sacred Presence as the Awareness, as kind-heartedness in the present.

You know this as your innermost self. When abiding in that pure perception, we abide as God's light, as God's being and his unwavering emanating grace. To believe this is honourable, but to be as it is, is the cornerstone of every spiritual liberation.

By being it, by experiencing yourself as this mercy of the freed soul, we can know God's true nature. So how can it be separated from the source of everyone's deepest natural knowing and perceiving?

God is everyone's and the one awareness of being.
God is one consciousness experienced as an indivisible
multiplicity of the infinitude of beings, ultimately belonging
to the one same universal existence source, oneness, unity.

Why cover it up? Why not bathe yourself in this eternal nourishing blissfulness of self-knowledge and the knowledge of the world? That holy bewilderment is the purpose of existence. That blessedness of universal comprehension, melting in its blossoming presentness, is the sweetest taste of being that any soul can yearn for.

Marry this freedom dear one, don't let it slip away within the ego's ignorance. Embrace the raw nature of the present moment and your life will be remembered and celebrated in the stars for millennia to come. You will carry a gaze and smile of youthful innocence but

possess the strength of a sage. You already and forever
will know this liberating prominence. You have always
and already chosen to remember and awaken to it.
You know you are it. You know there is nothing else.

You are the very presence as the awareness.

On the fundamental level, there is no separation
of consciousness, there is no subject or object.
There can only be one constant – beingness.

By experiencing and knowing this as yourself, you
know the only natural possible law. If we wish to name
it as something personal, call it God. If we wish to know
it for what it is, it is a Sacred Presence. And to be fully
real about this awareness business, we only need to
be using one inseparable term: consciousness.

Only when the mind is active and it
requires multiple sides of explanations,
do we name other instances of awareness.
Only then do we name it God.

When Christians say Jesus is the only way to
heaven, to God, they are right, because Jesus is the
pure consciousness or unconditional love, and these,
together with peace, are the only way, and the only
eternal truth as the self-aware presence of awareness.

*It is not about believing, fearing, or learning, but relaxing
into the natural ambience of awareness, into beingness.*

God is the one consciousness who gave us freedom
via our apparent individual point of attention, your
awareness, which is indeed extremely sacred.
We are all together God, and God is the One and none.
When you find yourself in the perfect peace of having
no thoughts, you will feel gratitude for this conscious
power we call God, this existing clarity of just being.

Beingness is the presence of awareness, a life of consciousness.

It helps, though, to point out different practices
that lead to more presence and being in the now.

PRESENCE PRACTICE

We are already full consciousness, but our awareness
is covered and distracted by thoughts, beliefs, ideas,
feelings, sensations and perceptions. As we don't and
can't create more awareness, consciousness or presence,
we can only allow it to be by peaceful annexation of the
mind. We do this by a gradual increase in awareness
of both our unconscious and involuntary actions,
reactions, addictions and urges.

Let's mention a few of those: smoking, sugar, gossip, narcissism, lovemaking, popular and social media, power, possessions, success, meaning and belonging.

Addictions, for example, are not harmful by nature, they are simply an action we cannot stop doing of our own free will. Let's focus on unhealthy addictions now, such as smoking or eating junk food, compared to addiction to health, which is even desirable as an alternative. Addiction is a shortcut to relaxing, relieving, or pleasurable experiences which we associate with a resulting feeling of happiness or pleasure.

Smoking is deep inhaling, relaxation, and a small glimpse into the present by stopping the mind for a moment with the release of dopamine. Awareness of breathing is the alternative and real desired experience.

Food addiction is about satisfying fullness in the stomach, relieving the discomfort of hunger.

We can heal addictions by remaining aware and slowly easing up on the need to satisfy them. In the present, our being is fully satisfied, apart from needing a bit of food and water. But the real spiritual food it needs is provided by awareness itself.

Our first intention must be to create well-being for ourselves first, for without it, how can we help others?

This includes doing the things you like, educating yourself, working on what you enjoy, and keeping your physical and mental health up in high spirits.

You could be stuck in life, with nothing to do, feeling like you have nowhere to go from this point. And it might become quite heavy and depressing to live like that. But, in truth, you are in the same position as most people who feel complete in a similar situation or even have less. They have learned to accept and enjoy their being, even if nothing special is happening in their life.

We should first learn to enjoy small, simple everyday things and find all the joy in them. This can be reading a book, writing, flowering, cooking, little bits of creativity around the house or garden, conversation, or just relaxing with a TV show or movie. Doing nothing and abiding in presence, however, can be the most rewarding activity. To be present is to abide in God.

By being aware of yourself, you are aware of everyone and everything else. You don't have to learn, but only to get used to presence as she is already fully here and is all that you are.

Consciousness is the one spirit, God. Awareness is a soul's way of life. A gift from God to all individual creatures, God's sacred blessing.

BEING WITH GOD

Every association with God should and must be welcoming and healthy for our well-being. It needs to be the source of divine inspiration and associated with the bliss of being in the moment, presentness and stillness.

God is a beautiful, short, and direct word and sound that describes and correlates with consciousness.

God cannot be subject to belief, possibility or chance. He is the conscious essence of our spiritual heart. This Spirit, power, force, much wider and greater than us, is comprised of awareness and is that from which we are essentially made of and are.

God and we are one, so why separate it with thoughts and doubts, when we only need to let go of trying to believe or not to believe to experience the abundance of God's presence? It is in this space and from such freedom that our love awakens, in the absence of fear, in knowing we as awareness, cannot die. Without the fear of death or end, what is there left to prevent us from being our true selves? It is this force of certainty into everlasting life as consciousness that allows for the occurrence of miracles. This brings us closer to the true purpose of organised society. There is strength in numbers and consciousness is infinite. Spirituality is waking up to the reality of such a life. But spiritual teachers would find the idea of an audience a bit funny because they see a divine presence in everyone. Conversely, what everybody thinks of themselves originates from these separate fearful entities that work and try so hard to maintain the idea and status of the self-important individual character, the story of their life.

People like to talk about themselves and others, they like to feel superior by comparing themselves, by seeing advantages or by finding any excuse to lower the opposition. They like to tell you all about themself, their heavy life story, the pains and joys, failures and triumphs. And it is all the ego talking and feeding on the listeners' attention. All the more if you can broadcast the story worldwide. This is the greatest form of embarrassment, instead of owning yourself and regaining your conscious dignity.

We have the responsibility to remain sane and aware, for anything less only leads to excuses and looking to shift the blame elsewhere. By giving away our freedom, our thoughts and our minds, we are giving up on our natural responsibility to take care of our own inner and, thus, outer spaces. No one can or should be in control of you. You must be the highest authority in your life.

Again, this is not about a man wanting to be a God, it is about a man just wanting to be a man, with full consciousness. It is only then, upon regaining your aware authenticity, that appreciation for existence will take precedence, and by doing so, you will truly honour the God who created it.

There is no sin in selfishness if by that we mean being full of ourselves, being ourselves, being the self by being selfless. A sin is a generalisation and simplification of the deeper psychological issue of unconsciousness or lack of necessities. Most actions that we consider to be a sin are preventable with proper education and when basic human needs are secured. For example, there would be no need to steal if you already have the things you wish for. The average citizen would never steal, it is simply below their moral standards. Of course, a lot of theft is carried out by rich people for the sake of even more wealth, power, and security, and their motivation falls under either a lack of moral discipline, addiction or a lack of spiritual dimension.

With that understanding, sin can be blamed on the culpable ones who haven't educated you, or provided an easy means to secure a livelihood. But mostly it is a lack of that spiritual dimension that underlies both material and moral aspects of necessities. It is on the responsibility of the system itself to provide such education. If we leave it to parents, well, we get exactly what we have now, which is negligence, as the parents themselves are improperly educated.

We should all have accessible means to free higher education, free housing and free travel.

Now, we cannot put all the sins into the above-mentioned criteria and disregard the possibility of some deeper spiritual and karmic involvement. But, given the wide spectra of misdeeds and the natural need to experience both polarities of existence, in short good and evil, there could be beings and souls who are unable to act differently. Such type of actions should be treated as evil and as purely purposeful ignorance. We call this a crime in the meanest sense, but it can go as far as being serious to the point of sheer demonic influence.

We should concentrate all our efforts on educating and providing sustainable well-being to the entirety of humanity, and, with that, evil will slowly dissipate, unable to thrive in a fully healthy and conscious society.

Just understanding this is not sufficient enough to effectively prevent sin or crime. Knowing how hard somebody has worked for certain goods could indeed prevent you from taking them. But if you know how much it will hurt them when causing hurt is your goal, this can also be your motivation for taking it.

Again, we have to develop that real sense of morality and spirituality that will prevent us from choosing any uncivilised behaviours.

Belief in God is not a good enough education either. For some, it is the exact opposite, a reason to commit a crime. We have to be realistic with our moral standards and refrain from living in a fantasy where there is an imaginary higher authority.

The police, army and law are real authorities, but their rules can differ and can also permit actions in one country that would be treated as a crime in another.

A similar analogy can be applied to many life situations across the world, and, for this reason, we have to come back to our most natural state of perception – pure awareness to educate and inform any prospect of a permanent solution to any problem, sin or unconsciousness.

We do this by staying firmly established in the moment, abiding in the natural present, and dealing with each arising thought, urge or desire by properly addressing their true cause, meaning and solution.

Now, that we have looked into the meaning of God as the sacred presence, which is our own awareness, let us investigate other various qualities and manifestations of consciousness, and learn how to recognise and access them.

Chapter 2

SPACIOUSNESS

Once you have freed yourself from all that is not serving your awakening self, you become free to look at the world in a natural way of a newfound space. We will call this newly open dimension of awareness 'spaciousness'.

In spiritual jargon, spaciousness is a term we associate with describing the properties of consciousness. And although it is a valid attempt, it is based on the sense of time and space, which are both merely illusory notions within the mind.

On the other hand, spaciousness is rightly correlated

with awareness as an infinite space in consciousness. So it is important to distinguish these two associations, as well as openness, which we will explore later.

There are, however, many more dimensions of consciousness, such as aliveness, wakefulness, and alertness experienced as boundless, infinite, unlimited, endless, etc. For this, we must point out and distinguish the difference between such awakening experiences of awareness and awakened or pure consciousness.

Personal experience of consciousness that we call awareness can feel like spaciousness and openness, but in non-duality, consciousness simply Is, outside space & time, so it doesn't feel like anything. In light of this, we have to ask ourselves who actually feels spacious or open, aware or peaceful. Or even more basic, common traits: who feels hurt, happy, lonely, loved?

The answer is I, as my state of awareness, as personality, as the sense of being myself. But the deeper truth is just being without any apparent individuality, the beingness, consciousness.

Seeing your nature clearly as a present consciousness and with that losing many, most, or all false beliefs, ideas, thoughts and emotional processes, will bring in a lot more space into your expanding awareness. And it is not that your awareness is really expanding, rather, it is set free from previously held sensations and perceptions.

In non-duality, there is no need for healing the past, for you are trying to heal the illusory memories of the idea of the person who itself is an illusion, an invention of the mind. It is enough to be still and notice the present blessing of life.

N<u>OW</u>

Before we explore the many dimensions of spaciousness, we shall first understand the heart of its meaning. This quality of present reality that holds entry to every association with consciousness is the now.

At the beginning of this book, we identified now with the present, but we have to further explore the most common misconception of the term the 'present moment'.

How do we perceive a single moment in the inseparable streaming continuation that is consciousness?

What we really think by the present moment is the now, and the now or present is the correct description or labelling of consciousness. There are no moments as such, same as there are no isolated thoughts, emotions, time or space that we can capture and observe. A moment is merely another word for the now, intending to focus or separate something which has occurred in the now.

Consciousness is an out of space & time beingness within which continuing stream of awareness is allowed.

Every instance of separating this presence of being aware can only happen in the now. In order to function in such separation perception, in the reality of multiple dimensions we even measure this and count nanoseconds in seconds, minutes in hours, days in weeks, months in years, centuries in millennia, etc. And to hypothetically measure the now, we have called it a moment.

None of these measurements exist though. They are navigational mental tools to enable us to make some sense of reality, of the apparent passage of time, to make life easier to understand, organise, plan and navigate. So they are very useful tactics to deal with practicalities in every way, but we do pay a price for involving our awareness with it. We get lost in time & space.

If you imagine yourself in complete darkness, in the centre of the universe, you would instantly feel the lack of time & space. And you can try this in any dark room without a sound. This also makes this the perfect ambience for meditation. As soon as we are cut off from our sensory perceptions, we are left only with our sense

of presence, with our undisturbed awareness,
with pure consciousness.

Here we are in the present, in the now. But we
can not measure a moment, as even our thoughts and
emotions have settled and left us with nothing to hold
on to, nothing to think about. Without experiencing time
& space, we are left with no two points of reference to
refer to it as a moment. We only know of the presentness,
of infinite spacious awareness.

If you are to return to the earth, you would have a
profound insight into the underlying nature of reality.
You would lose a need to count the moment, to measure
time and would instead be immersed in the immense
space of the now, the present beingness, spaciousness.

This is exactly the experience that we need to free
ourselves from the added illusions, to abide in
the basic reality of existence, in consciousness.

We will, however, keep using the term 'the moment'
throughout the book, but it will clarify this distinct meaning in comparison compared to the usage of 'the now'.

As you learn to flow with your awareness, there
is more space and more time available for you. You
prioritise your life in a different way now. You are not
a slave to addiction, drama or control, so you can let go

of all those mind traps and all the ego games so you can be dedicated to the new you in abundant space.

Now you are more interested in the spiritual dimension that outlasts all the mental and physical attachments. You have stepped into spaciousness.

You are genuinely concerned with others' well-being, for you know that every soul has an opportunity to shine its light as it is naturally intended. But also, now you take care of yourself and your mental, physical and spiritual wealth. You are not a victim of circumstances, you take your destiny into your own hands with a newly freed mind and newly allowed spacious consciousness.

Now you prefer silence over noise, books over TV
and nature over religion.

Now you understand why the mind clings to all the distractions, why media is popular, why ego prefers troublemakers over peacemakers, and how religion is claiming rights over the prophets, of God, dictating the narratives of faith. Now you can clearly see how governments and corporations are led and instructed by world organisations to indoctrinate and control humanity. But, in truth, we are allowing for this manipulation by complying with and even supporting the Status Quo.

But as soon as we make a conscious shift of expanded awareness, we begin to influence and change the unconscious structure by creating a more sustainable, spiritual and natural way to live.

An aware person sees how our life is inextricably linked to nature and how we are dependent on nature to keep civilisation going. Such a person cannot ignore this obvious connection, and they embrace the natural world for all its worth.

Therefore, it is not a rarity for spiritual teachers, activists and entrepreneurs to establish communes and well-being centres in nature to inspire and show how beautiful and symbiotic life with nature can be. Leading by a healthy practical example is the way for a new earth community.

SPACE

Spaciousness is all about the feeling of having enough space around you or, to be more precise, inside you. A conscious person can indeed function perfectly normally in a small or enclosed space, they can survive a lifetime in a prison cell without feeling confined or lacking in space. And this is exactly what mystics do once immersed in pure consciousness. They spend a long time sitting isolated in caves so that nothing can disturb their lasting absorption in the bliss of the present.

In such a state of no thoughts and no perceptions, they do not perceive time or space, they do not see walls. Inside their boundless space of awareness, they feel infinite and completely free. And walls really serve to allow for space. Space is the main reason for building walls. We build walls and houses to capture space.

In light of this, give yourself some space, to work, to live, to move, to be. The only thing standing between you and the infinite space of awareness, is your mind, in other words, your thoughts and feelings.

The mind is like a veil over consciousness, limiting our awareness to whatever it decides to think or however it decides our body will feel through our emotions.

But consider animals and vegetation, matter, air or water. Nothing is preventing them from being one with infinitude, we only see them as separate due to their visibility. But the appearance of all these is already one with the infinite, with the space surrounding them.

They do pay a heavy price though, as they are not self-aware, or aware of spaciousness. They exist as nature's program, which is almost equal to nonexistence.

And this is where you come into play, where your self-awareness and the awareness of the infinite space around you is the true blessing of existence that is being self-recognised and self-realised through its conscious agents, namely you, me and all of us humans.

All the natural world is, however, a great teacher, as it shows us how it exists in symbiosis with itself, unaware yes, but fully integrated into the circle of life, and most importantly of all, not troubled by thoughts.

So you too can move around like an animal, fully engaged and absorbed in life itself. You too can sit silently like a tree or a flower and be fully aware of your surroundings, completely at peace in the moment, growing in good health with a natural demeanour.

You too can be one with the space around you, with no thought, by solely appreciating the miracle of existence through the virtue of beingness. You are the aware witness, you are the space in & around you, and you are the blissful allowance of the most natural recognition as the sacred presence.

It is when we allow ourselves to experience life through such pure mercy of heartfelt perception, that our inner grace awakens and liberates us from missing the present moment, that sacred centre as the awareness.

This is not about practising some abstract spirituality, but it's about letting go of what is no longer serving you and feeling into the natural presence with your innate consciousness.

It is the healing process of coming back to self,
your true self, one being fearless in abiding as awareness.
One unswayed by the world's temptations of ignorance
but inspired to bring some long-awaited sanity and
kind-heartedness. Such awakened presence nourishes
all those who remain lost and hidden behind the masks
of pride or shame. But there is nothing to be afraid of
once you let go of the societal indoctrination into
all kinds of behavioural stereotypes.

Listen to me, without you, there is no awareness
of your particular point in consciousness. You exist to
awaken to this miracle of self-recognition and abide in a
middle way. Within yourself, you have the capacity to be
fully centred and aware, and there are only so many of
us privileged in the eyes of existence in this particular
universe. So allow me to help. Take my hand of truth
and we will lead ourselves into the sweetest freedom
with our higher self.

NATURE

To expand your awareness, one needs to remain aware
and clear of thought. To clear thoughts, we gradually
practise remaining in full awareness. We do this through
stillness, peacefulness, focus, alertness, and relaxing body

and mind. Above all, the practise is contemplation followed by meditation.

We can also stay in the places where our mind will be less prone to engage in thought, such as the peace of our room or the wide natural landscape.

Staying out in the open terrain can feel like a natural return to awareness. Anything related to nature will catalyse awareness. If you can venture into pristine nature, absent of any human involvement, this environment promotes immense peace of mind, more than any spiritual attempts in the city could, for instance.

There is primordial tranquillity embedded in nature that human beings feel innately connected to. If nothing else, the natural spontaneity and sheer beauty of nature can trigger returning to our natural awareness, compared to the mechanical and concrete feel of cities. Above all, nature will give you space to be and, with that, freedom from thinking.

If I were to suggest only one thing to you that will awaken more awareness and more of yourself, it would be to go out camping in pristine nature alone for several days or for as long as you can.

Go to the place in nature where you feel a natural pull to stay, where you would like to remain aware.

This place has to be free from human activity,
such as structures, roads, human noise and passing cars.
It needs to be quiet, it needs to feel free. Such beautiful
settings will correlate with your true spacious self, your
pure consciousness. Within moments, hours and days
in this natural space, your mind will ease into a state
of complete, focused presentness, fully at peace.
Here you don't have to do any practice,
as nature is doing the healing herself.

This is natural meditation, staying in the
authenticity of your true self, feeling independence
and solitude. In such calming, you find your
conscious freedom of the universe.

Be in nature, seek out that feeling of timelessness
and experience the peace and tranquillity of the land,
the freedom to move, to feel, to be and, gaze upon the
reality of Earth in its natural state. Allow it to settle you
in its presence, to sway you with its tempo. Let it anchor
you in a place of nourishing, nurturing mindfulness.
Your mind empty of thought but full of awareness.

All you need is there, embedded in nature.
You are nature coming home to your
natural place of timeless space.

Be open like the sky, vast like an ocean.
Be enormous like the universe and infinite like existence.

Be the space without tradition, patriarchy or hierarchy, the place which only nature provides. Embrace nature in its fullest expression. Escape the system's deadly routine. Notice aliveness in nature.

We have grown accustomed to living in secure cities with many people never venturing outside the city limits. Yes, sure, they go to a park or visit the zoo, but these are no comparison to the sheer enormity of experiencing wild, pristine nature. We have grown so feeble in the face of the world's reality, hypnotised by societal corporality. To wake up from this mirage of individuality, we return to the one natural global feeling of freedom.

This is spaciousness inborn, manifested through your human form, by remaining consciously aware of the primordial sacred space, being one with God and being free at last.

You will become profoundly aware of many consciousness dimensions and correspondingly abide in the flavour that you have come to experience on Earth the most. You will notice the evolutionary force of biology and the incredible growing power of vegetation and trees. You will be humbled by the presence of so much natural space, the awesome force of climate and weather, which play the main role in environmental and biological lore.

Here, you will surely realise the magnificence of
it all, the existence of atoms, molecules and cells as the
building blocks of universal creation. You will be amazed
at the very phenomenon of organic life, at the countless
shapes & forms oragnisms develop into.

Above all, you will fully achieve your own self-
realisation as the awakened consciousness of the world
and universe. Of the transcendental implications that
such freedom brings, alongside the immeasurable
responsibility that such self-aware aliveness truly brings.

We can build and change the universe with it.
Tempering with the very circle of life and death, of not
only ours or even stars, but of existence itself. With the
gift of self-mastery, we have been given the keys to the
divine throne itself. We can become Gods in the image
and likeness of our choosing according to our beliefs
and projections.

This awesome power has surely been used before,
to create the universe and allow us access to it.

So whether we will stay humble or be proud in the
face of this opportunity, in the face of our self-realisation,
is yet to be seen. Even though it is obvious that this
struggle has already been fought for millennia,
it is especially prominent in the world today.

But the very nature of the world and the universe
is openness, vastness and space, an endless welcoming

space of possibilities in being creative, ingenious and resourceful. Just like space is open, nature is open and it requires space to grow, spread and flourish. As an aware extension of nature, we need only to leave her some space, follow her earthly beat and stay connected to our own beating hearts of prominence and stillness.

You, as an infinite space of awareness, the pure point of consciousness, are here to even the odds and let the shining glory of the one beloved source prevail in its natural spaciousness.

Spaciousness is the freedom in which and with which consciousness or God can interact with existence. Spaciousness is the Spirit of existence, the beingness. So to look at it from another angle, spaciousness is the quality of self-realised awareness. Similar to how 'the spirit descending unto you' spaciousness is the space and blessing of being aware. Like sunshine, it is always here, without any need to create it. Just allow it to be, naturally present and aware.

To allow yourself space to live and be is important in order to welcome in the awareness of yourself and consciousness.

Nothing in life is more important than your conscious presence being in and appreciating the raw reality of nature. For this reason, the greatest conscious progress is the complete experience of freedom in nature.

As previously mentioned, this means going to the natural environment where you don't see or hear any human activity. And take nothing modern yourself, with a paper and pen as the exception, and spend a day, or two, or three being free like that. Forget about work, people, TV, the internet, the world, spiritualism, and, most of all, forget about yourself. These are all false associations, confusing at best. But what does matter is your awareness itself, pure, each moment born with the wisdom of ages. Freed infinity.

By being accepting of the immediate experience, the first thing you will notice is elevated happiness resulting from this newfound freedom from habits and addictions. Your mind will stop. Your attention will have a single focus with a gaze of presentness. Your soul will fast realise its value as a conscious agent, a being capable of movement and reason. But above all, one is fully immersed in divine perceptibility of what is actually here, now, raw and real.

Nothing unreal exists, nothing real persists.

This utmost return to the true self is your ticket to a paradise of never skipping a moment, the eternal now which is etched and immortalised as nature itself.

Chapter 3

OPENNESS

WONDER

Where would you go? What would you do? What would you be, If you had absolute freedom of movement, time, and space? If you had an infinite awareness of each & every moment of experience? How would you behave? How would you treat others? And yourself?

How would you treat the earth? Would you go back to nature? Would you go back to self, to being self-aware?

Or would you deny it all, blowing up the chance to achieve self-mastery? Pass the moment as unwanted?

Stay in the comfort of avoiding the now, instead feeling uncomfortable with any instance of the present or sanity that the beloved can bring, when truly you can feel so safe and at home by embracing the moment.

In giving no resistance to the present, your being will persist as consciousness. Just by relaxing your body and staying open with the natural stream of awareness, you have done more than kings and generals through the ages. You have performed miracles just by being still. You have allowed for life when others have denied it. You have taught the truth of eons when others have written Bibles to mislead. You haven't touched a rock when others have moved mountains for their glory's sake. You have cherished the sun like it is a god's son when others have hidden in the shade.

The son is natural luminance, enlightening the mind with the light of illumination. So just like the real sun, find yourself most often high in the clouds, contemplating existence.

We know we will all die, we will all perish from this world within decades. So what does this understanding teach us, what does it mean?

Use the time that you do have, the time that is now, to abide in the universal comprehension and from this open space of knowing awareness, manifest a reality you wish to experience on a daily basis. There is only a lifetime of time to waste or to use it.

For what if you found yourself in the most extraordinary circumstances in the most ordinary place? Your open spacious awareness. Then, time won't matter anyway, for you will have accessed the transvaluation of all thoughts and emotions, in simple abidance by consciousness. In that silent ambience where the noise in your head turns into a pleasant standstill of the mind. When there is no character left to thought and play. When all the world disappears in the monumental peace of the present. When all that remains is your sacred presence as awareness. Then you will finally fathom the secret of the universe. An absence of thoughts, a pure consciousness. A mystery so long and vast, it evades almost all people. So profound a state, that we consider those who embody it to be gods.

But you don't become a sage by self-proclamation. It is others who put it on you when you start speaking and living such an awakening wisdom of the graceful heart, concentrated mind and penetrating gaze.

Time is of the essence when seeing there is no time at all, no concept of the future, no memory of the past. By remaining with your present wisdom, you have unlocked a holy grail of beingness itself. Such is the will of the universe, to reward those who neither want nor ask, who don't even think or feel, but those who know outside a 'stream of consciousness'. They benefit from aligning with conscious awareness.

Openness is a quality of freedom in being but it is not necessarily always associated with being open to society. Some realised awarenesses prefer to stay almost entirely isolated from other people and the rest of the world, to be fully immersed in their being, while some keep functioning in society exponentially. Here we can see the traits of the soul's personality and consciousness' individualistic nature. Generally, one opens to their innermost being first and then relations with the world are in the space of possibilities.

In the realisation of non-dual existence, awareness is left purely as consciousness, and in such a perfect state there is ultimately no need or reason to do anything. This is because everything is perfectly relative in the ultimate nature of the universe.

It is our mind that sees and needs to interact and control the world, but the world is an expression of the universal state of being. It does not need the mind's involvement. However, the mind will be involved as long as is necessary to realise itself as consciousness that will enable the surrender into being. This is a so-called evolution of consciousness, but, in truth, consciousness doesn't evolve, the mind does.

All words aside, the beauty of awakening is meant to be experienced and felt. As indescribable as it is, seeing a clear golden sky as a window into heaven itself after long, depressing rains could almost come close to putting it into words. Or feeling like you are riding in a chariot of every imaginary dream of love and tenderness manifested on white shining cumulus clouds, bathing in an infinite pleasure trove of being one and whole again.

Welcome to the paradise of the eternally observed moment, where you'll repeatedly witness sights truly being worth being referred to as remarkable, phenomenal and extraordinary yet are as simple and natural as the open awareness of being.

FEARLESS

When looking at the totality of human life experience, its pleasantness is primarily determined by the amount of fear we hold within. So whether you will be happy or sad all comes down to one's level of fear.

Most of our fears and problems can be solved by remaining in a peaceful state of being, which is our natural stillness.

We have turned the most natural faculty of conscious-ness, which is a state of being aware, into something to achieve, work on, practice and heal, when all that is necessary is simply a present recognition of being.

I am not writing about some extraordinary state that will have you levitate and possess superhuman powers. I am relaying the simple presence of being. Which is in the now, found in the stillness of your natural awareness.

As we grow up, most fears become irrelevant. We can notice how they were just small feelings of unease due to unknown territories or situations. Venturing into the unknown is therefore a very good way to deal with fear. Whether it is being amongst new people or in new places, such as a new work environment, landscape or city, once we get used to something the fear will dissipate accordingly.

Furthermore, we can attribute most of the facets of fear to the fact that we care what other people think or will think. People are often nervous around new people, dealing with problems or when speaking in public. But the most widespread fear is for our immediate survival. At the very least it is the fear of what might happen tomorrow or in the near future, undoubtedly, is based on the daily grind and having the means to live.

We are constantly worried about our job security, whether we are earning enough, about our health, our car breaking down, paying the mortgage, providing an adequate quality life for our family, what will happen if we get a divorce, what will become of our children, what type of person will they become, what future do they have, if the weather will affect us, where our country is heading, the economy, environment, the world, the meaning and purpose of the universe, of life and so on...

The only way to deal with any issue is to remain present and open. Either to deal with the problem or by diving deeper to see that there is no problem at all, other than the mental one. And we could separate all these fears into two categories: physical and mental. With one being the catalyst for the other and vice versa.

Fear results from believing in our separate selves, mixed with the belief in time, which gives us the illusion of life and death, and that is the only thing that we are afraid of. We are afraid of dying. You see how mental belief is the main protagonist in our life, and this belief includes believing in the reality of the world. All this slowly develops during our upbringing within the system. We are moulded into these human material entities whose view of the world becomes almost entirely materialistic. We are trying to solve the problems on a material level when the real solution would be a mental one. For example, repeatedly buying new toys will not solve children's issues, but will only postpone them in exchange for greater consequences. The solution for children is to spend quality time with them, interacting, playing, educating and, most of all, creating an open space for them to move, learn and grow their spiritual, mental and physical health.

Remain open to your treasured being while it is slowly expanding together with your heart's beauty. You have to see it for yourself. You have to feel and dance with the openness of the one. You have to allow yourself to melt in its blossoming soul. Be excited because you are an inseparable part of it. You are the significant peace of the whole. Your worth is not somewhere in future success, or anyone else's acknowledgement. Your worth shines with the power of infinite existence, all expressed and centred through your glowing present awareness.

You are here, permanently. Period.

Your open awareness is a link and gateway to the treasures of blissfulness that are forever accessible in recognising each moment as the eternal now. What a tremendous gift from God it is, to be consciously open and aware of the universal existence, to be aware of you, to be aware with you. It is your presence that keeps the world going in so many unique ways of being & feeling.

And still, we share the world with so many natural miracles that are beyond our imagination. Our coming of age is a continuing process that is as vast as all the stars in the multiverse, where each universe, each speck of light and matter dances in a tantrum of holding the potential for self-realisation. A flowering beauty of a blooming lotus soul.

Openness is about opening to the possibilities
of an infinite self, present as awareness.
It is a mark of genius with traits of a sage.

You will be entertained, you will be educated and you might become awakened by following your heart. Your heart is freely flowing when you allow it to be, expressing its soul values to restless minds or forgotten hearts. By opening yourself to its loving influence, you open the door for others to walk in the footsteps of the giants of kindness.

Open your lungs to breathe in the full natural presence of life. Open your mind to expand your intellect into a funfair of imaginary nows. Open your body's energy field so that life can take you on the journey of belonging to any part or sight and nature scape in the world it deemed necessary for you to experience. But, above all, keep your awareness open and present so that you may enjoy every moment of beingness on this wonderful earth.

Isn't life beautiful when you choose to be open and still, witnessing the minute details and grand vistas with each sacred presence as your awareness?

HEART

Openness is an inherent quality of consciousness that we also interpret as unconditional love, as being the Yes Man, as positivity, the bliss of life, the inspiration to be at the core of truth, as reaching out, volunteering, doing humanitarian work, nature conservation, protecting animals and being devoted to the source from where one abides in the sweet nectar of gratitude and selflessness.

Openness is non-resistance to the moment. It is awakening into the highest self and manifesting one's destined bliss. It is seeing reality as it is while being fearless in abiding by awareness. It is being centred on the heart.

Openness is the spark of life that makes us alive. By expressing our innermost sacredness, we are sure to stay in the attitude of freedom and health. For being oneself freely is what heals us at the core of our psyche and soul.

By being open, we allow the natural flow of the universe and that is God wanting you to explore your fullest potential. In seeing the bigger picture of the world and understanding everyone's path to discovering their true self, it is only natural to be openly accepting in the light of one's own self-realisation.

> *Openness is a merciful state of perception,*
> *a constant falling into grace, into kindness.*

To be open is to be in love with the world, to love life, and wholeheartedly embrace your conscious existence.

In experiencing many paths by being open, we learn that only by staying positive and true to the awakening cause, can we influence others' lives in the right direction of bringing abundance, peace and happiness to the world. We do this specifically by loving, acting from love and melting the ego layers of society's long-time closed hearts and masked faces.

You and I are the ones with the already washed-up hearts, faces, and souls, as we humbly, but proudly, ascend into the promise of liberated awareness and openly embrace the sacred spirit.

> *Openness is like a breath of fresh air,*
> *a constant feeling of warmth kept alive*
> *by staying true to your unwavering heart.*

Be open to the infinite possibilities that life can play out in relationships, family, work, entertainment, culture, art, creativity, science and religion. Go with the flow, don't force the routine. And once you are tuned to what the universe is trying to express through you, once you have relaxed into listening to what & when you want something, allow settling in that newfound liberation of routinely going with the flow of transcended inspiration.

Open your intuitive wonderment and allow yourself to be touched by holy sacredness, vast inner space and a spiritual heart that knows fate, hope and love. One which endures petty trivialities of materialistic small-mindedness that instead expands its vision beyond the shores of this visible world, to speak and teach of the unsung kingdoms of freedom and soul strength.

This holy fire of elegance lies within each brave heart that has been yearning for a life-changing call. Those who answered and led armies of angels were once just a part of a greater whole. But the road to heavenly glory is one of self-righteousness and utmost dedication to that unmistakable vision of what true paradise means, for it is in each moment of full conscious breath that we are forever reminded of our true illuminating purpose.

Openness will spiritually inspire you to abide in the sacred space of presence. Fuelled by the wisdom of the source essence, you will remain focused and invigorated to the sharing of bliss.

Always a good omen, with the blessing Amen.

In our reality, Jesus stands as the purest example
of living with an open heart. He is the embodiment of
openness as shining awareness in the deepest expression.
His birth was human and his character is that of a sage,
but his living essence is transparent – it is divine.
And how else would God behave awakened in
human form? It would be a sight of grace, timeless
wisdom and a fearless expression of oneness.

Jesus can be found in the openness of a heart where
acceptance of being lies – God. This heart recognises a
soul in need and it approaches them with its capacity
to nurture and heal. Such compassion, such care, is
the gentle awareness that also acknowledges all of the
natural world appreciating a flower, a bird, an animal.
It takes a rest against a tree and speaks to those
assembled about the light of being.

Jesus is not just some historic person, he is a universal
quality of love: the Christ consciousness. Just as Buddha
is the epitome of stillness and wisdom, which are traits
of oneness, Jesus is an enlightened awareness of purity
and love. So too, God is recognised as the most general,
universal, fundamental quality of being, which is
awareness and your awareness of it.

Without awareness there is no you, no knowledge of God.
Without you there is only consciousness, there is only God.
Your naked being as consciousness is God.

Consciousness is known in the individual as awareness, presence, present, being, God. All these terms indicating beingness really describe the one, only ultimate quality, the only reality, which is the one consciousness. Whatever the type of experience, in whichever spiritual dimension or material reality it is, we only ever know it through consciousness by being aware.

Be open, like a welcoming friend, never expecting
a prize in return for giving a helping hand,
sharing a heart or teaching with a pen.

Your treasure has been already collected
by self-rewarding deeds of what is right & just
in each moment of the fearless act.

You only have one life to either mess up
or choose to be kind, for everyone is fighting their battle
between sanity and reasoning over being kind
or making excuses to not be nice.

You only benefit from those you have been beneficial towards.

And we benefit by knowing they are alive in
spirit and well in their hearts.

There is no need to leave anyone behind to
dwell for another lifetime in their cognitive dissonance.
Literally, everyone can be reached by heart-to-heart
interaction and be saved in present togetherness.

In this overwhelming ambience of embodied selflessness,
where freedom overtakes pain and openness is the medicine,
the blossoming flower lotus petal heart awakens a beauty
of the soul that God has bestowed unto you
including everyone else who presently abides.

The euphoria of crossing the sea of lostness to
arrive on the opposite shore of consciousness
is called the bliss of being in the moment.

And you too, my dear human,
can remember your universal origin,
the star that bares the name of your soul's heritage
and, upon fully regaining consciousness
can stand in awe of the blissfulness
of each openly recognised moment.

I love you and send the most heartfelt Namaste.

Chapter 4

STILLNESS

Awakening of the human soul and consciousness encompasses a variety of subjects. The main subject is how we become aware of inner stillness, which is in our most basic nature and is an essential part of any civilised society. Without it, we are merely slaves to our unconscious yearnings.

True accomplishment is a man's spirituality, his relationship with consciousness, awakening the freedom to express his love and share it with the wider world. And that starts with one's own family.

Stillness allows us to observe and control ourselves fully. For instance, animals, for the most part, are incapable of doing that. They are primarily driven by their naturally inherited behaviours and almost predetermined evolutionary reactions. They are simply unable to resist their basic urges to move, feed, rest and procreate, doing what nature evolved them to do. We can say with great certainty that a lion will always be a predator and the antelope will always be prey. This is set in stone by evolutionary biology.

But one branch of primates made a huge evolutionary leap by developing complete self-awareness, completing the entire circle of consciousness. Human beings, therefore, possess the ability to control themselves, observe their natural urges and do virtually whatever they want with them. This can and should be practised in a state of peace with both the mind and the body.

It is largely through meditation that we can enter perfect stillness and, in a way, experience leaving the body and the feeling of abiding in pure beingness. By lifting ourselves away from base perceptions, we are inevitably stripped of their limitations. The result is an absence of fear plus the presence of freedom that is found in limitless eternal awareness. What other sense has greater power than the knowledge that there is no death and that without death eternal life exists and is present?

The best way to utilise and allow for stillness in one's life is to become aware of one's inner dimension of being, namely consciousness. This is primarily done by being aware of our breathing, and with this comes a direct experience of the free and aware space that is naturally present in each of us. In doing so, one also begins to recognise their timeless, boundless nature as conscious awareness.

You are awareness, a point in consciousness, constantly engaged by perception and sensation, yet, present nevertheless. This perpetual, natural presence is enduring, constant and ever-present, but it is involved in a world of movement, clouded by thought. You cannot create more awareness as it constantly streams from being to knowing. You can not reduce it either, as it is effortlessly flowing without beginning or end.

The only thing you can do is know yourself
as awareness, as the knowing of being.

To add anything more to this innate recognition of one's presence as awareness, which is fully complete and satisfied by every conscious moment in the present knowing, would be to overwhelm the simplicity of your natural attentivity. One would lose oneself in the complexity of unconsciousness that constantly yearns

for the sacred knowledge of existing by feeling safe
and peaceful in the here and now.

In remaining free from attaching to thoughts, notice
an underlying peacefulness as well as overwhelming
presentness. Although we like to refer to this as an
expansion of awareness, it is not so much an expansion
but, rather, a contraction of awareness, a coming back
to a natural state of undisturbed consciousness.

Allowing yourself to rest in its eternally welcoming
sensation of presence – your pure consciousness – is the
sweetest nectar of stillness, living at peace in abiding
bliss. The clarity you perceive permeates a quality of
instantly recognising the source, the underlying being.

You can simply stop looking for something,
stop seeking it and stop needing & desiring it.

Instead, become aware of the transcendent peace that
is presently here, as your awareness of consciousness.
Be open to that sacred peace, don't resist it, and don't
cover it up with noise and constant mental & physical
involvement. Let it be, free and open.

Complete stillness is the entry point
to feeling nothing and
being everything.

PEACE

Stillness is an inner shrine of peace, the place of rest
to which your mind surrenders. This peace will bring
you so much more peace. The only thing you really have
is your own piece of peace. Your own piece of God,
of one consciousness.

This could be the simplest way to abide in stillness,
but it is certainly not the easiest. It seems that the easiest
way for humans to find peace and solace in stillness
is in the fulfilment of chasing happiness.

For example, as children, we want food & toys,
and we are at peace and satisfied while the experience
lasts, which is not for too long. As adults, we want to
achieve a career and have a meaningful family life, and
we are at peace while the stages of these ambitions are
fulfilled until we feel the pull to gain yet more fulfilment.
Such is the nature of seeking peace of mind by finding
happiness in objects, relationships and meaning.
But that is a mind trap, the systematic game of
playing real-life Monopoly or The Sims.

The next possible way to find peace in stillness is to
surrender to God. This is not simply to believe in God
but, rather, to feel the experience of surrendering. There
is a huge difference between thinking that one believes

in God and the experience of this spiritual dimension of losing yourself in God. To feel relieved from yourself, from the burden of ego and living with it, is profoundly powerful, so much so that more than half of the people on Earth claim to be religious or to have an affiliation with God. But to base your well-being on faith alone, on God as an outside attribute, truly requires a leap of faith, since faith is usually accompanied by a corresponding amount of doubt.

In essence, God is pure consciousness that has been translated into words and further clouded by doing. Because of this, we must seek that original taste of divinity in the authentic experience of one's own unceasing awareness, which is found in the silent stillness of our natural, untainted sacred presence.

Furthermore, when people have given up on life or are lazy, they tend to think that this means they have found peace. But this is a form of resistance to our natural being, which can move effortlessly with the flow of life, making it capable of any feat of doing by basing itself in being.

In short, if you don't have the will to live, you have not found peace, but the rejection of being. Depression and laziness are signs of unwillingness to live, which is a direct resistance to being.

In contrast, to truly find inner peace in one's stillness is to enjoy being, even when faced with adversity. Hence, hardship has never been shown to be able to touch the radiating awareness of one's sacred presence.

The soul thrives on being, not on doing or experiencing, for this awareness feels pleasant in any type of engagement. It can feel good in heat or cold, in happiness or sadness, in joy or pain, in doing or being.

Finding peace in stillness is the natural way for consciousness but it is not limited to it. Inner stillness is therefore not a subject related to the state of the world or the fate of one's life story, but it is naturally present and pleasant in awareness.

We can find the source of most of our problems in our lack of stillness, such as worry, stress, jealousy, hate, insecurity and so on. All these are felt like a sudden surge of unpleasant energy within the body or even a prolonged feeling of discomfort. That manifests as a sick feeling in the stomach, a heartache, headache, nervousness, sweating, fear and even crying.

Frustration of any kind is also a very common sign of restlessness, especially frustration associated with the global unconsciousness of humanity.

All of these symptoms are side effects of distress.

We can calm and heal these problem by abiding in true God's mercy of our sacred presence. This is, as we have already mentioned, accessed by the stillness of aware breathing enabling the recognition of our true nature as a deathless spirit in the freed space by. As such, we are stripped of our fear and have the courage and divine inspiration for the heart-to-heart interaction with every being we encounter, which also includes the natural world.

It turns out that the simplest peaceful way is the only way after all.

All these examples show how important or even crucial it is to be constantly present and aware of one's presence. You could be taught how to be still, but you can only be still by being aware of your conscious presence. So what you are really learning is to remember that you have to be fully aware of each moment. You remember that you are present but, mostly, you notice the natural stillness that is fundamentally here, underlying as consciousness.

If you want to avoid a lot of seeking, wasting time and losing money, I advise you to simply become real, right now and attentive to the present. Don't let another moment pass by thinking that you are not fit to know yourself as the sacred presence that you are as the awareness. You only ought to be still where all the time will be narrowed to only the space of your present.

I can only direct you to become aware of your own space where the answers to your life await. You don't need another book, you don't need another teacher, you don't need more time or understanding. You need to have enough presence and will to abide by the natural stillness which is always here and now.

Stillness is always the first answer to every question, whatever the question might be. After that, whether one chooses love, peace and action, or blame, hate and violence, is entirely up to circumstantial and unconscious forces. But stillness is the entry point to any interaction or abstinence.

Everything must have started from one, oneness, consciousness. These fundamental qualities can not be separated or divided, but they do dream within themselves about the other. So the universe was created, a cell appeared, then cells and all further life.

You don't have to rewind the entire history of the universe, escape all dimensions to realise this or yourself. Just as when watching a movie, you can simply press exit and shut down the storytelling. You do this by remaining still, allowing thoughts to settle and being the one consciousness again.

This is the greatest thing about consciousness,
it allows for the entire history of the world to unfold,
but there is a safety exit installed with it, a kill switch
for dreaming and liberation from unconscious fate.

Find that place of peace. The peace that will stop
your resentments, jealousy towards the rich and pity
for the poor. Find the kind of peace which flirts with
love when looking at the world. Find and hold on to that
beautiful heart knowledge that everything is running
its course, and don't portray the arrogance to change it.

For how dare we correct God's great non-dual plan
with our circumstantial existentialism? We, who whine
about self-righteousness to those who neither have food
to be full of themselves, nor rights to learn about these
consciousnesses. When we only need to abide as the self
and be righteous in an egoless way. Our pride is quick to
cast judgment and condemn another human being but
is slow to notice the source of the noise of internal
commentary and greet the living essence of their soul.

Because of this devilish internal and, in no lesser
degree, external dialogue of the ceaseless self-talk,
the world has been spinning on the axis called I. I, I, I,
me, myself and mine, are every mind's favourite words.

They could be thrown out of any language without ever changing a line. Yet here we are, going around in spiralling circles of karmic lifetimes while bathing in the attention of every missing me & I. We are driven by immediate needs and desires. This makes it challenging to focus on bigger, more meaningful goals, as we are less likely to abandon our comfort zone and invest further.

Stillness can help with both. It can settle you in peace and free you from being bound to comfort, or it can bring peace in a time of need. Like Buddha, stillness is a doorway to a tranquil being. It can open up your spiritual heart by calming the ego and illuminating the mind. It can help you with sexual instability by returning you to your natural conscious state which is far less dramatic and needy than what modern culture portrays.

There is no doubt that the main reason for biological existence is the need to feed, shelter and procreate. But in the human world, this has been pervaded to the point of addiction and obsession. We are slaves to our hunger, comfort and pleasure. The majority of humanity is merely only indulging in those basic evolutionary urges, with no moral or spiritual ambitions.

We, humans, are indeed intelligent animals with awesome conscious capacity and capability of being fully self-aware. But in the state of blissful arrogant ignorance, we have turned Earth into a giant agricultural farmhouse. We are a hundred years overdue with our planet's destruction, desolating the countryside to feed a hundred billion livestock so that we can eat meat.

We live in concrete, steel and glass jungles. To the sane, natural and conscious person, the world is a madhouse of unconscious civilisation. And, somehow, we have convinced ourselves that we enjoy this illusion.

We work jobs that we don't like to pay for the house we spend only a few hours in, mostly serving the needs of our children who will likely end up in a bad relationship with both us and their own partners, and the wheel of karmic life whose only product is the destruction of our environment keep spinning.

No wonder most philosophers have concluded that such a life is meaningless and that the true meaning lies in having a sustainable relationship with nature to preserve it. Top that with transcending soul values in art, culture and infrastructure. This makes for a stark comparison with aimless consumption and addictive satisfaction.

Further, we don't have children to better humanity, we have them for social and emotional comfort. We don't eat to feed our bodies, we eat to stuff our stomachs and quell the feeling of hunger. We don't live to engage our mental and spiritual capabilities, we live to remain lazy in both regards.

Still, half of humanity claims religious or spiritual affiliation, but this does little to change their basic behaviour like being rooted in consciousness does.

Yet this is the obvious evolution of consciousness into self-realised awareness. Ultimately everything is perfect, but earth-wise, we might not be here to witness our own true nature as present awareness.

We are, however, able to regain that freedom right now, through our conscious effort of simply being relaxed and present.

In not holding on to anything, nothing can own us, therefore we are free.

How much more peace and beauty there would be in the world if more of humanity awakened to this inner light of awareness and acknowledged everyone's shining presence as valuable as our own, and more.

Here lies an inexhaustible peace and tranquillity that will have us utter wisdom of ages, the heart talk which will inspire generations for millennia to come, as did Jesus and Buddha upon taking the path of righteousness.

*You too can overcome all the obstacles
that are preventing you from abiding in
unalloyed happiness, Ramana has said,
it is your natural state, an inherent trait.*

Chapter 5

ꓘOTHINGNESS

Since consciousness is a superposition of possibilities, it is safer to call it nothing, rather than everything.

Nothingness is therefore its prime state, the nothing out of which anything can manifest. In the same way that the black TV screen holds the possibility of showing any imaginary play with all possible scenarios held within itself, so too does consciousness.

This nothing, out of anything can come out of, is the basic state of all things. It is consciousness, ultimately known by our awareness and is further manifested by one's intention.

When you close your eyes, there is nothingness,
just conscious presence. When you open your eyes
there is something or everything suddenly experienced.
We cannot escape these basic states of perception and
being. They are the canvas upon which our life plays out.
And whether it will be steeped in ignorance, indulgence
or self-refinement is the mystery we are addressing here.

Given all this, we find it necessary to talk about both
nothing and everything within the same context, they
are the two faces of the same coin and one cannot exist
without the other. One is nothing, the other is something
and both are comprised out of the same consciousness.

Understanding any aspect of consciousness is about
stripping away the reality of perceptions, to its very nature, its fundamental state. And how else to know what
nothingness is, without experiencing nothing? Whether it
is in the form of owning nothing or holding to nothing is
up to you. Some people can learn from others' examples
but most need to taste it for themselves at least once.

Nothingness is best understood in the literal state
of nothingness. Having no relationships, job or agenda.
In a way, it is absolute freedom, which doesn't mean
security. When Jesus went to the desert, he experienced
nothingness. When Buddha left everything and went

into the forest, he experienced nothing. When Ramana settled, absorbed in being, he experienced nothingness. All they had left was pure consciousness. But after that, they returned to a somewhat normal life spiritually. They learned what they needed in that ambience of complete surrender to the purest experience of being.

To be purely conscious is to know nothing. To experience nothing doesn't necessarily imply full understanding or awakening. Millions of people have nothing daily, and, for them, it is just another day of suffering unless they get used to it and are even happy. But they are certainly not consciously illuminated or transformed spiritually by the experience. Nothing is all they know but they stay oblivious to the pure beingness.

To experience its real essence, any negative connotations must be removed from the idea of nothingness. You must want nothingness almost dearly to have an authentic insight.

In nothing, everything is contained as a possibility.

Be aware of infinite nothingness and manifest any life dream you have. In knowing nothingness there is no fear left. Without fear, everything is possible to achieve. And what better wishes are there than bringing

happiness into people's lives, for the preservation
of nature and to create a sustainable future?

When you are left with nothing, life suddenly allows
for everything. It is a gift for those who have surpassed
themselves.

SOMETHING IN NOTHING

Nothing and something are interrelated, in the sense
that one cannot exist without the other, nothing can't be
without something and vice versa. To determine space
& time, a point of reference is needed, a measurable
dimension. The same principle applies to something in
relation to nothing and nothing in relation to something.

These qualities are the base of existence as physical
entities, as matter in space. To talk about nothing is
ultimately discovering everything, all the possibilities.
Nothingness is only a prelude to somethingness.
These are the existential dancers of consciousness,
within the apparent universe.

In other words, the person who enjoys the peace
of nothingness has already experienced enough of
something and found contentment in the silent space
of awareness. But for as long as we know, the masses
tend to appreciate the noise makers more and avoid
peacemakers due to the mind's need to be involved in

entertainment and substances.

If we, however, want to survive the challenges facing us on the planetary level, we need to allow ourselves more awareness in order to develop the increased level of intelligence that is required to achieve this.

We all have the same awareness, we are all together as one collective consciousness. Everyone's spark is light, and everyone's part is equally significant. In staying true to your deepest self, you are ensuring that you are contributing towards the inevitable assembly of the source essence, dissolving unconsciousness into presentness.

Nothingness or emptiness is most commonly associated with Buddhist teachings. Once the mind stays still, it will appear to be empty, to be nothing, to be at peace. But such a state has negative connotations attached, since identity and character got lost together with the mind, the world tends to be perceived in a relative, flat, same or indifferent way. It may be seen as nothing, even if one is perceiving everything. And it is the fascination with and addiction to everything, to the 'ten thousand things', that holds the mind in service to both the ego and the endless involvement in the world in its bid to seek out happiness.

Nothingness is synonymous with consciousness and, therefore, has been incorporated into the essence of the

Christian message, as the way of poverty and again in Buddhist teachings as the impermanence of all things.

It is also apparent in all other religious, spiritual and modern practices, such as fasting. The proverb 'Man does not live by bread alone', is true since consciousness is always and fully enough for itself. It needs nothing to survive, it thrives on nothingness since it is empty and is made only of space itself.

Here, the ancient tradition of sungazing bears relevance, as surviving only on the Sun's energy is a much closer example of the truly spiritual life. Mana from heaven would be another example.

If you still think that all of this is far-fetched, don't forget that we know matter is merely an illusion, matter is just the way our senses decode existence. Matter is entirely empty, so we feed on the idea of food only, as with any other material substance. Life is merely a dream that feels real thanks to our minds which tend to trust and identify with external stimuli.

In popular culture movies, *The Matrix* and *Inception* have explored this recent scientific realisation, which mystics have been describing for millennia. We are the Spirit, inhabiting a Soul which animates a mind & body.

For awareness to progress it is obvious how we need to experience and then jumpstart the currently incarnating level of life, which in our case is the third dimension. To return to the spirit, the soul needs to experience the body, the physical world and then transcend it via the means of self-realisation.

This happens as awakening, illumination and, finally, liberation. In practical terms, it means waking up to the fact of being self-aware, and with that seeing the illusion, the system, lies, manipulation and ego, while also noticing all the beauty in life, nature, love.

In light of this, one follows their highest excitement and fully becomes their highest self, illuminated by the light of consciousness. And finally by experiencing one-self as a deathless spirit, enquiring on their true nature, one abides permanently as pure conscious awareness.

These three stages in one's self-recognition are only the most commonly reported experiences. In the same way that as we have three main meals of the day, the actual experienced truth is much more complex, or more simple than that. We could have many more meals and snacks in a day, or we don't have to have a single one.

It all eventually falls into a conscious space of nothingness. You only need to enjoy yourself while it lasts or scrupulously enquire into the self. Either way can, will or won't work. Consciousness will decide.

NON-ATTACHMENT

Being accustomed to nothingness can help with addictions and holding on to things unnecessarily. It is common knowledge that wanting or desiring something is the root of all suffering, which Buddha revealed, so being content with nothing is a stepping stone towards freedom. But even if we want or desire nothingness, this can be an ego-driven way to remain in charge.

Spiritual attainment is often based on a person's wants and needs, mainly the desire for freedom and happiness.

By aligning with nothing, it is far easier to experience owning nothing and appreciate receiving something.

The point here is that one need not be afraid of having nothing, especially not fearful of thinking nothing, for the only true liberation is found in complete freedom from possessions, whether mental or physical. Only when the mind stays still, when we think, feel or do nothing, can we be truly liberated in consciousness.

Our world is civilised, busy, modern, progressive and it doesn't follow minimalistic principles. We are forced to rent or own some form of living space, we are pressed to own a car and strongly urged to further invest in real estate. It is obvious how much we have to adjust spiritually to this so-called civilised way of life.

Instead of trying to be ascetic or mystic, we need to understand and practice the principle of non-attachment to material things. It is acceptable to own something, but it is an attachment to it that causes suffering. We need to see things in their essential nature, as nothingness, so that we can use them free from attachment to enhance our lives in a more fulfilling, yet still practical way.

With non-attachment it is possible to remain calm in the face of any loss imaginable. If you lose a car, house, partner or child, or you suffer from a much greater global catastrophe, you can stay centred in your aware being in the event of any such shock.

You know the ultimate fate of the universe. You know we don't live forever in a human form. You know physic-al things get destroyed. You know that things can happen in one's life, often unpredicted, but you can cope with any event and stay calm with your fully present being.

A great loss is usually attributable to a tragic event, but it is the greatest lesson in disguise, a lesson strongly anchored in the present that demonstrates how holding on to something hurts. It teaches that there is a clear choice available between suffering loss or moving on.

After the loss, people often feel liberated and light, for the loss has proven to only be a great burden of which one is now free. And we can see right now the true nature of our interactions, relationships, ownerships and attachments. Right now, we can choose to be free from any unhealthy or unrealistic connection. In fact, this is the only thing we need to do in life: stay free of people and things, even if we own or are related to them.

Jesus said it is easier for the camel to pass through the eye of a needle than for a rich man to enter the kingdom of heaven. He meant that is impossible to be fully conscious if one owns possessions. And the truth of that can also be seen in the lives of Buddha, Ramana and all the mystics who abandoned all possessions either before or after self-realisation.

Still, it is okay to own, grow, manifest, create and ease your life. It's okay to progress together with the world. It is our destiny as apparent physical beings. But we do have a psyche, and we do need to train it with our soul strength and spiritual intellect.

In having everything you can,
know the meaning of having nothing,
and in holding on to nothing you can
be free when owning everything.

Non-attachment, therefore, is the key to a contented, but even more so, a truly present and satisfied life.

In non-attachment, we find peace and ease of mind every day, in every situation, purchase or investment.

Life is an experience, but you don't have to take things so much to heart that it hurts when the inevitable happens. Simply ask yourself what type of life you want to experience. With how much ease do I want to perceive everyday occurrences? Will it change anything if I keep holding on to what was or what I don't have? Can I remain abiding in the pleasant ambience of awareness?

I am certain of two things. First: years will pass, life will shrink and you will find yourself in a position of lateness, unable to do what you wanted, so do what you want now.

Second: I know nothing other than consciousness that lasts forever, so why invest my well-being in a passing experience? The answer is as present as the knowing of your very awareness.

As conscious agents, we have to presume that this state can be taught and reciprocated, that we are not only victims of the universe but free, conscious participants as well.

This premise stands at the core of our lives, central to the existential mystery, where nothingness is as good as owning the universe itself. By this, we're not only a drop in an ocean, we are the ocean in essence. Every conscious point in the universe comprises the entire whole.

Again, this is not about our own pride but it is about being boundless as the consciousness that we are. So after all, by having nothing we benefit as though we have everything. In staying small we secure our greatness.

True spirituality is not about being good, helping others or being devoted to God. It is about reaching self-realisation by freeing yourself in consciousness and discovering that it is who you really are.

In some advanced world, there is no poverty, nobody in need of help; everyone is provided for. The only thing in such a best-case scenario would be to deepen yourself in awareness, ultimately in nothingness, the base of spirituality and existence.

INDIFFERENCE

It has been said that 'there is ultimately nothing ever happening, reality is an illusion, the matrix is real, space & time are doomed, before everything there was nothing, out of nothingness everything emerged, the universe is a hologram, what a beautiful day, God is'.

All these types of statements indicate a merging with the infinite, with the divine, a realisation of how there is no separation or action, but complete uniformity and perfection of being.

So, is nothing better than something, or is it better to ask if something is better than nothing? Relatively speaking, it doesn't matter to consciousness. Existence was free of the universe for infinity and it was doing well without it. Earth was devoid of humans for billions of years and it did very well without us. Consciousness did not blink in the process.

For 200,000 years humans have been developing and for thousands of years, they've spread to dominate most of the landmass of the globe. Would it make any difference to the universe if human civilisation were to collapse and disappear from the Earth? Consciousness wouldn't care.

We know the disappearance of humanity would be a huge relief for the natural world, which would overtake, overrun and overgrow agricultural fields, roads, cities, seas and housing. Within decades most of the visible signs of humanity would be hidden. Within a hundred years it would have completely disappeared and melted into the environment. It would take thousands of years for certain products and materials to crumble and dissolve, but they would be hard to notice anyway.

There would be no aware humans to witness this miracle of nature, but consciousness would not care.

One hundred years is a mere lifetime compared with millions and even billions of years that nature has on its side before the sun swallows the solar system and returns something into nothing. Consciousness still wouldn't care.

It would be very interesting to witness nature reclaiming human space. Witnessing nothing quickly growing and multiplying into something would almost be like watching the last centuries on rewind. But consciousness wouldn't care.

It would remain indifferent to the comings and goings of the universes. It would stay silent in the face of the birth and death of so many creatures, beings, lives. It wouldn't flinch at the sight of changing so many forms & shapes. It would remain in blissful knowledge as undisturbed beingness.

Once we do find peace of mind, we may seem oblivious to the rest of the world, but nothing could be further from the truth, we are fully aware of it.
We are, of course, no longer identifying with the world. We know that the world's everything is

ultimately based on nothing, that it was born from nothing and that it will inevitably return to nothingness.

The Big Bang is the mother of this understanding and the father of our universe.

The ways of consciousness and the destiny of the universe are unknown. It depends on our intentions to make sense of it all, to give meaning, and find purpose in an ever-changing world of timeless consciousness.

And whether we end up with nothing or with something, we are due to surrender to the eternal nothingness out of whose mysterious path something can always emerge out to live, do and abide within again.

Chapter 6

ℭONSCIOUSNESS

Consciousness is beingness within which our awareness is present. Ultimately, these are all terms pointing to the same knowing within ourselves, but since we do experience different types and levels of perception, we need and want to be as accurate as possible so that the recognition of the ultimate truth is closer and more likely to be realised.

Here, consciousness is the ultimate foundation upon which all other sensations happen, and it is the one knowledge by which we can be sure that we are made entirely of her.

But the moment we say her, we need to drop the idea that it is nameable or titled and remain in the noticing presentness. We could say it is feeling and knowing experience, rather than thinking or believing. Although it is possible to know it intellectually, the spiritual goal is to be it, as it is the only thing that we are. So by this understanding, it is not separate from the very life that you, me and entire existence are. We are that presence.

We have to and will return to it, and we will realise our destined purpose as the sacredness of each and every moment of experience.

Such a state of pure innocent perception based on consciousness will liberate our stranded minds from restlessness and ignorance. It will lead us on the journey of awakening to return to our truest selves: at peace, being silently present and aware, without resistance, but enjoying this pleasant peacefulness, this constant wakefulness, this fulfilling emptiness, nothingness, this safe openness.

That peaceful awareness is the backdrop for all the noise and action. It is the holy silence that permeates existence with its ever-present consciousness. It is God, Spirit and the Sacred Presence as the Awareness.

Truth is eternal silence, the presence it is.
Consciousness is, the inevitable return to silence.

Every attempt to describe any of this is, by definition, inadequate or even wrong. Human language can serve only so much as to point towards it, but the final experience of this aware freedom comes only by the virtue of authentic stillness.

In truth, any language is a signpost, but it is not the bliss itself. For this reason, some realised beings don't write or even say much, as such is the nature of complete liberation. There are really no words that can describe illumination, no language by which to fathom awakening. That is why self-realisation is the most sought-after experience or state, why it is so rare for one to achieve it and why it is so transcendental to one's core being.

It all comes down to knowing yourself as awareness in every moment of experience and acting from such liberating authenticity, which is the illuminating love of the one beloved, one source, one essence, one being, oneness – the fully realised self.

Of course, we shouldn't be discouraged from attempting to describe and write about this state, this truth, this ultimate freedom. We shouldn't be discouraged from acting, creating and sharing from this liberating inspiration. On the contrary. This state of complete fearlessness is the one togetherness that can influence and transform society into a sustainable livelihood.

We are each a precious soul yearning to be liberated from the routine of a daily grind and catapult ourselves on the journey of spiritual fulfilment.

Daily healing is the process by which to start and accomplish our innate vision of what true paradise encompasses, to bring such lasting self-perseverance and happiness to all who seek to free themselves into collective radiance.

Such attributes of the soul are always and already alive inside of us. Fear is what prevents the soul from being fully realised, with the catalyst being the ego, the mind.

So I welcome You again to free yourself from limitations and blame, as we are all in this together, and even though most of us will never meet or cross each other's paths, we only need to be truthful with the ones we do see and interact with.

Consciousness is our being,
and a blissful soul is our life,
let's decide to honour that aliveness
in each of us and greet everyone
we meet with a joyful heart.
It is where our true essence resides,
where our soul forever abides.

KNOWING

Consciousness is not an existing phenomenon,
but the beingness within which existence appears and
becomes aware of itself. It is the constant and present
background of all beings. By saying 'constant', I also
mean without beginning or end, without birth or death.
It is the one singular knowing. By 'one' and 'single',
I mean not separated as it is not even oneness but
unaccounted for. Like space, but spaceless.

Consciousness is an entirely unique quality, so there
are no correct or exact words in existence that can be
used to effectively describe it. For this reason, it has
always been describing in the East using negating terms,
by saying what consciousness isn't, rather than what it is.
Intellectually, we can only glimpse at what it is, even
though we are it. The secret to knowing it, is to be it.

Again, to describe it is to be poetic, with all due
respect. But as we have seen so far throughout in
our four books, I enjoy trying to describe it anyways.

Let us now look at some of those negating ways
of dealing with consciousness.

In Vedantic tradition, this is called the Neti Neti
process, or 'not this, not that'. This is done by
disregarding everything one can be aware of

as not part of oneself, before coming to the true self, simply the awareness itself.

Buddha has also used only negative terms. He would say what consciousness or awakening will take away from you rather than bring you. For example, meditation will quiet your mind and, consequently, you will lose depression, fear, desires and problems, but what will remain is undefinable.

In other words, consciousness is unspeakable, therefore not touchable, approachable or visible, not temporary, measurable, nameable or separable.

But I wouldn't say that consciousness is unknowable, incomprehensible or non-understandable, for we are in, out and from consciousness. There is nothing to us other than consciousness. It is our first, simplest and only nature. We are it, we are from it, we are in it.

Consciousness is the only thing we can and do know.

Everything else is fictitious projection, imagination, belief, thought or felt emotion. Consciousness is the only ever-present quality of our being, so how could we not know it? We do know it, and we know it without knowing it, and without trying, for it doesn't require an effort to be itself.

Consciousness is closer than close to us, so we don't have to try to know or understand it. We let it be, us, as it is, because it is as we are.

Consciousness should be the only thing that we should talk about because it is the only thing that is. That's why spiritual people, for the most part, are only interested in these conscious matters. They find little interest in mind games. They enjoy being and they like to be free, abiding in this infinite space of inner knowing that we call consciousness.

We could use the term 'awareness' synonymously with consciousness, but it is easier to say that we are aware of something. Aware within and with consciousness. It comes down to personal preference over which term to use. Society has already established labels to describe specific conscious functions, which are mostly correct and are the reason why it is so easy to talk about consciousness in the West today, despite lacking a long spiritual tradition such as the East has.

There is no need to travel to the East to study these subjects. All you need is to find your perfect centre of stillness and let the East come to you if it wishes.

There is no need to find Buddha, for he is already here, behind your eyes, as a fully conscious gaze.

There is also no need to seek Jesus, for he is your awakened love. Consciousness doesn't travel, it is Here and eternally so. Once Ramana has realised his true nature, he remained in the same place for life.

Oh, how I wish for this transcending peace to hit you. To settle your mind and allow the experience of pure consciousness. To give you a taste of your true being, of beingness.

Allow yourself enough space, enough stillness to realise yourself in it, and you will become one with everything. In such freed-up, unrestrictive space, there will be no thought, no intention to speak, move or think, only the radiating goodness of being.

I advise you to meditate until you feel so completely immersed in such freedom that it becomes your constant habitual state. As such, you will no longer need to formally meditate.

We should be taught how to invoke this natural state in schools from a young age. Children ought to be supported in being accustomed to meditation, peace and quiet, since in such state they will be empowered for the rest of their lives to engage in real, meaningful conversations, creativity and existence.

This inherent peace would eliminate any need for

religion, spirituality or politics. We would simply
come together when necessary to agree on the best,
most natural solution to any problem. No ego,
no self-seeking, no national pride, no wars.

The most recognisable trait of consciousness
is peacefulness and acceptance.

As an all-being, consciousness pervades every atom
and space with her unceasing presence. For this reason,
every place matters the same, as there truly ever is
only one space of infinite awareness.

Consciousness can not be cut. It is not divided into countless
points of awareness, it is always one, unseparated whole.

We only seem to perceive through an apparent
separate awareness due to the illusory appearance of
the experienced dream that we call life. Einstein referred
to it as an optical illusion of consciousness.

We don't personally have one piece of consciousness,
rather, we feel an illusory sense of separation.
We perceive 3D, a narrow spectrum of visible light,
which is just a tiny imaginary reality in comparison
to the actual infinite state of possibilities that exist.

But this life and reality seem so real that we disregard
our scientific observations that which do inform us there

is no matter as such, we are creating this dream
with our presence alone, as conscious observers.
In other words, matter only exists when awareness is.

Without apparent awareness, consciousness abides
in the state of unmanifested stillness, where no singular
scenario has been pulled out of an infinite state of
possibilities.

Now we too can abide in such a state of pure,
unmanifested potential. It lies in perfect stillness,
where no thought can touch us. Here, there is no us
as awareness but a clean presence of the eternal now.

It is the state in which existence exists in its
dimensionless state, before the birth of the universe.

We are truly in this state always, we just imagine
something else, we dream of this universe, and we
are born in this human form to learn about ourselves
as the source of the projection.

We, thus, are not projected, we are its source.
We are not looking at it, we are the looking itself.
We are not manifested but the catalyst for manifestation.

To arrive at a complete standstill is to become aware
of the world. To inquire who is looking, who is being
aware, is to realise the self of all that is being looked at.

This awareness that only remains, that you are.
This infinite space of awareness, the knowing that it is,
is the ultimate knowledge, the secret, God.
This undisturbed, unfiltered presence that we are, God is.

Existence is a river of time freely flowing, and our awareness is an estuary of imagined dreams. The same analogy can be applied to every growing organism where our desires are veins of the tree, and manifest order in the greater scheme is a canopy. One avenue of discord creates & inspires the other. Like an evolution of thought, awareness branches out in a multitude of streams, so much so that it requires infinity to fit them all in.

To stop acting and reacting, to reason and realise, to remain abiding in one's presence of awareness is to wind down from the tree, from the stream of constant anticipation.

As prime consciousness, you are here to do just that.

When no time comes, when clocks stop ticking,
you find yourself in the knowing of your being, as it is.
Present, unborn, but complete.
Neither eternal nor yet conceived.
All knowing yet without trying or understanding.
Unlimited yet one.
Not two but oneness.
Existing as its beingness.

Consciousness is not all, yet all comes from it.
It is not everywhere, but everything is in it.
As she can't be cut, we know there is
only one consciousness experiencing
itself as countless myriads.

We don't have consciousness,
we are of it, in it, it.

We cannot fight, argue or philosophise over this truth.
It can only be noticed, recognised and acknowledged.

To compare this with the actual experience of reality,
a belief in God is undoubtedly a belief in a supernatural
being, but if you still think that consciousness is also
just another belief or replacement for God, you do not
understand it as you are still enslaved by thinking.

Consciousness is the knowing of your self-awareness,
it is the return to real reality of existence.

You cannot think to comprehend this.
You cannot access it with your separate, clouded
awareness, you have to be it to live it. You have to
experience it and know it deeply. Then you can be
sure of its nature, and you can talk about it with the
certainty and credibility of personal experience.

The easiest way to give you a taste of the difference between human awareness and pure consciousness is to show you. For that, simply turn to the next page and stay with it for a while, contemplating obvious conclusions.

What did you feel?

The written pages represents human activity, localised awareness, while the blank page is a state of pure consciousness unmanifested. It is spaciousness, openness, emptiness and nothingness.

And I can assure you that God abides in that space of non-creation. It is not him that is talking to you. What is talking is some other manifest consciousness, some universal soul that feels divine.

But God is forever silent and still.

God = Consciousness.

These do not need to speak, create or even exist, for they preceded existence. They know not of the subject-object relationship. Where they are is no space, time, point, no dimension and no words can describe it.

In the mountains, where I mostly enjoy trips into nature, there is a small Buddha statue. Nobody knows about it so it feels special. And every time I go to visit him, he sits unmoved, perfectly silent and still, lost in the natural surroundings. But from visit to visit it is obvious how much I have been running around, with both my mind and feet. You see God is exactly like that Buddha,

contented in the serene bliss of being, immersed
in the present. There is no effort to be or not to be.
There is only beingness.

Jesus was often immersed in deepest contemplation
and prayer remaining concentrated for the entire day
or night. Even when walking, the blessing of being
was honoured in peaceful meditation. When he felt
like teaching, he spoke. When there was no need to,
he remained silent.

All beings who honour consciousness are
sitting and walking with God.

HAPPINESS

Freedom and consciousness are synonymous.
There is no need for things or for another if one is truly
free. Freedom is about being real, authentic and natural.
These qualities are what an awakening soul tends to
naturally be drawn towards.

It is not about being happy, which is a feeling; it is a
temporary burst of relaxation from the constant tension.
However, our natural state is freedom and peace.

Notice that we don't eat to be happy, but merely to

put the feeling of hunger at ease, to provide our bodies with the necessary nutrients. Eating doesn't make you happy, it makes you relaxed and satisfied.

We don't make love to be happy, otherwise, it would be a continuous act. We do it to put our urges at rest. Making love doesn't make you happy, it makes you relaxed and satisfied.

We do experience that moment of dopamine which translates as the moment of complete relief. We felt a lack and in the moment it feels alleviated and satisfied, a short laugh or smile results. But what truly remains afterwards is relaxation and peace until the lack or urge arises again, due to the chemical, material nature of our bodies.

We have to provide our bodies energy in the form of food and pleasure in the form of satisfaction.

We don't buy a car to make us happy, we buy it to make our life easier, faster, more effortless. Sure, it could provide us with moments of joy, but most of the time we simply enjoy the benefits of using it. So enjoyment doesn't even make us happy but it does make us satisfied, as the nature of pleasure.

But there is a far greater facet of the needs we have as humans – the need for meaning. And this is a mental and spiritual form of lack.

Here again, we don't need a book to make us happy, for example, but to be informed and to put our mind at rest once we feel we know enough. People will read newspapers every day, read online blogs and posts, and watch TV news or YouTube videos to stay updated with the latest celebrity gossip or current global news. In one way or another, this makes them feel like they belong as part of civilisation.

Furthermore, the need to have a family is not about happiness but fulfilling societal purpose and living your life in a meaningful way.

The scope of such purpose and meaning goes much further if you do humanitarian or volunteer work and is much greater than personal happiness, if at all. Rather it is about the ultimate meaning of being a fully realised human soul.

Happiness is really more of a general term we use to describe the overall feeling of satisfying a certain need. But it is far from being a constant state or even being real. For you have to ask yourself who or what is feeling this happiness or sadness?

It's merely the mind.

Happiness doesn't come from doing but
from the appreciation of being.

Doing something makes us melt into being, and
that focus on the present brings peace, joy and happiness.
Losing yourself in just doing for the sake of doing robs
us of being. And again, being aware of doing
brings us true joy.

Become aware of doing by surrendering to being.

From personal experience, I can say that I don't do
anything for the sole purpose of making myself happy,
I do things to also put my mind and soul at ease.
This is the primary reason why I feel a responsibility
and need to share these awakening insights with the
community and the world. It is simply fulfilling
my true purpose on this earth.

There is always a specific reason for doing anything
and, the more real we become, the less it has to do
with happiness and, more with overall contentment,
peace and one's true purpose.

I can therefore confidently say that I don't even want
happiness, I want peace. I want to be real. I want to be
true to my awareness. And for that, I don't have to want
any of this, for awareness of peace is already here,
naturally present. This is the greatest realisation:
true freedom. The knowing that we essentially
are and have what we though we were looking for.

You are already the joy, happiness and peace that you were out there searching for in substance abuse, relationships and satisfaction. All we have to do to abide in this realisation is to be silently aware of the present. To be an unmoving Buddha, a contemplative Jesus, the silent Ramana, all of whom are expressions of God manifested.

GOD CONSCIOUSNESS

People want God because they need something to grasp on to. When all other methods of chasing happiness are exhausted, God is always there as a final refuge. And so people often remember or turn to God when all else has failed them. But what or who is this God they think is out there waiting for them to call out to him? Where is this being who answers prayers?

The answers are: he is not and he is nowhere. He is the awareness of the seeker themself.

You will need God and be 'Waiting for Godot' for as long as you are unacquainted with yourself as the fully present consciousness, the sacred presence of awareness. Until then, God is a useful master and a legitimate figure of a heavenly father. God is basically us in the future, once we have ascended the ladder of illumination to escape the cycle of incarnations to continue progressing towards liberation to eventually remain one – God.

God is that infinite, wise presence, the highest authority. God is the real angel keeping you safe on your journey of self-discovery to finding your and his divine presence. And consciousness is the centre, the intermission of that trip, keeping you anchored in awareness.

And, sure, you can get lost on the journey, but only concerning knowing which path to take. There is no one path to God, yet every conscious endeavour leads to God, as it is rooted in awareness.

For most people who believe in God, that sense of God is not actually present. They only believe and think about God and consequently feel the belief, but such a God is a result of tradition, reasoning and a lack of knowing oneself. And here we are addressing that deeper aspect, the sense of God's presence.

It is important to take note of how both being inspired by God's love towards man and the realisation of one's consciousness both awaken similar qualities in a person, such as a lack of fear, a feeling of being loved, knowing that everything will be alright at the end, deep appreciation for all beings and animals, recognition of nature, the gift of eloquence, true wisdom and the unconditional love of an awakened heart.

God represents all the most valuable qualities of a living being, while consciousness is all the qualities of beingness. For society, God's attributes play a more essential role as they are closely related to human values. While consciousness is of a universal existence, it serves better in transcending the human and looking into beingness itself.

God is about involvement, consciousness non-engagement.

Christianity is the appropriate religion to celebrate God while Buddhism acknowledges consciousness. There are no wrong and right efforts, only circumstantial priorities in the greater scheme of things. God is playing a vital role in the development of human awareness towards the realisation of pure consciousness. We are all playing our parts too. Let us make our roles worth remembering, inspirational and awakening to one's soul.

Once your soul is fully functional and alive, it is only a joy to share it with others, whether in a material or spiritual way. And what greater gift in life is there than contributing to others' soul development?

Spiritual work is a union with God,
manifesting your true purpose on this earth,
experiencing the real beauty of
being a conscious social entity.

Begin with focusing your attention, the ability to remain in control of oneself, to be still. This state of inner silence is where the true wisdom comes, the knowledge of sacred presence. Prayer such 'Our Father' honours such peace by inviting us to dedicate ourselves to the one supreme source, God.

This means being conscious and not excessively bowing to the in ego, but abiding in the serenity of one's awareness. In accessing your inner beauty, you step into the blessed feeling of utmost care for the now, for the beings in your vicinity and, thus, for the wider world.

Healing the world starts with an individual self which translates into every action towards a sustainable reality.

Creating well-being is as important as conscious bliss, especially if the latter is evading you. You must have a comfortable job, preferably doing what you like and owning your time if possible. Relationships must be a match made in heaven, otherwise, life can turn into a living hell. The place you call home must feel like a true home where you feel safe and enjoy living. Finally the being itself, on the continent, in the country, city. If you feel uncomfortable with yourself, with the life you have created, then you will suffer and struggle with unconsciousness. An uneasy life means an unsettled mind. A pleasant life allows for peace of consciousness.

We can observe how in developing countries, lack of education in all areas leads to a more localised state of awareness, one based on securing only the basic necessities. And consciousness primarily thrives on freedom, time, peace, intelligence and the global understanding of civilisation and the universe.

Education and development are therefore prerequisites for the expansion of global human consciousness. Although consciousness fundamentally doesn't depend on intelligence, but on awareness of itself, education, together with experience, lead to heightened awareness, which can allow for the free flow of consciousness.

Experience without reason and understanding is stationary, observation with learning is progress.

Unconsciousness needs experience and reason to regain and remain in the natural state of awareness to be pure consciousness. It requires observation of the present, noticing of being, attention to the now, focus on the moment and an awareness that is being aware.

It is from naturally experienced consciousness that morality and spirituality come forth. It is from that knowing of being that we access true intelligence, understanding, and constant awareness of the present.

In such a state of present awareness, our being feels sacred, healed and complete. It naturally radiates the goodness of being, as there is no resistance left for the present moment. The now is fully accepted and enjoyed. In this state of awaring, you know consciousness. And once you know this is the only thing that really is, how can you dedicate yourself to anything other than consciousness?

By merely observing oneself, you are witness to the greatest magic in existence, the miracle of self-awareness.

How privileged are we to be God's favourite!
How lucky we are to be at the top of evolution!
How responsible it is to be spearheading
the evolution of awareness!

We are at the point where awareness looks at itself in the mirror and knows itself as consciousness. You could be the last person on Earth or lost in masses, but you will always know yourself as consciousness. You can only be aware of yourself and your surroundings.

And this is not work. There is no work involved in being conscious, as consciousness is effortlessly stream-ing awareness. We surrender to its presence and allow for its natural perception of existence, the beingness.

How wonderful is it to know this secret to the universe!
How amazing it is to be! How beautiful it is!

Chapter 7

*A*WARENESS

WHAT IS AND WHAT ISN'T?

What is reality? What is real as opposed to unreal? How do we know that we are real? How can we be sure that the impulses in our brains are not artificially stimulated? After all, how can we know that we have a brain to begin with?

Unfortunately, I cannot give you the answers to these intriguing questions. However, I can point out something more important to you, more fundamental and far more significant. It would be to ask the correct question:

what is *the knowing* itself? And who exactly knows, when referring to, *I know*?

The answer is conscious awareness.

Awareness itself is the one undeniable quality of the being that knows, that is aware. Awareness is aware of knowing, and awareness is aware that it is aware. Awareness is aware that it is awareness. In fact, by knowing oneself as awareness itself, one inevitably knows that one can only be awareness since only awareness can know itself as being aware. Also, by abiding as awareness, one notices that knowing as awareness doesn't cease. Therefore awareness is unobscured by what it notices, since the knowing of itself never ends. It also never starts; it is a continuum.

Awareness' knowing of itself is therefore the one constant faculty of beingness, the consciousness that is.

Awareness is the light that hits a target, streaming from consciousness which is the flashlight. By our very being, we are shining the light of our awareness unto the world. Without one's awareness, consciousness is lying dormant. So to exist awareness must have a reference of time & space, of dimension. And once it falls asleep, it rests as undisturbed consciousness again.

If I were to ask you if you are present right now
and if you are aware, what would be your answer?
There is no doubt that you can only give the positive
answer of 'yes, I am aware'. And we really shouldn't look
anywhere else for the confirmation of one's awareness
than in such direct present observation. In truth, this
is the only possible case. We can know ourselves as an
aware being only in the present moment, only in the now.

We shouldn't be using intellect here, or memories, but
the certainty of the present experience. Life is happening
now, and we know it with awareness, that's it. That is
the reality of existence. That is the state of the universe
as beingness. Such is the nature of the world based
on awareness. This is basically all that I know.
This is, with certainty, everything that anyone can know.

Now that we are sure how awareness is our constant
state, we need to further notice how awareness isn't a
personal quality, but a conscious and open space. It is not
that you have awareness, but you are awareness itself.
All that we think we are is changing and temporary,
but the awareness by which we know thoughts,
feelings and perceptions is constant. There is
nothing else to us other than awareness.

We are not aware. Awareness is aware.

There really is no such identity as being human. Any idea and sense of personality are nothing but a construct within awareness. It's true to say, we are all aware, but we are not all aware clearly, of our true nature as awareness. Most people somehow completely identify with their self-image as a human having experiences.

For example, people think they are male or female, but there is no such thing as gender other than physical anatomy. All else is a mental construct and a belief of how males or females should behave. Naturally, we are born as male/female reproductive biological entities, but not as a woman or a man, which is an artificial image created by society. Awareness is neutral and is sheer presence. There is no female or male awareness, there is only awareness. Maybe our soul has some gender-associated polarity, but the spirit is genderless.

People identify with the colour of their skin, with their race. But, as with gender, race is only a biological variety, it doesn't come with a fixed racial identity. Again, these are mental constructs. Awareness has no colour, it has no race. Awareness is only aware of the variety.

In addition, people build their identity on the region, country or continent they are born or brought up in. They identify with the religion and culture in which they are raised. These, again, are many chances and flavours of civilisation, but they are all occurring in awareness and can be influenced and changed by education and life circumstances. They are all witnessed by unchanging awareness. We can easily imagine being born in any other country, having any religious beliefs, behaving in any style and living by any cultural code.

But above these experiences, we can always remain presently aware as neutral awareness. Not identified with any particular sense of self, but being peacefully present of our conscious essence.

People take huge pride in identifying with absolutely anything because it gives them a sense of belonging. We are primarily culturally conditioned to do so.

We can continue relentlessly with a vast array of identities, altered states of self, beliefs and personalities, all of which are misidentifications of ego. This entire life and system are a huge game of survival, fun and searching for a sense of belonging. And all is merely confusion within awareness. It is all an illusion based on the separation of playing societal roles.

But what would happen if you simply remain consciously aware as awareness, and not identified with any of the mental games? What would happen if you decided to be still and present? Do you think you would lose something? Are you afraid of holding onto nothing?

There is only infinite awareness to gain and limiting fears to lose. It comes down to how real and true to yourself you want to be. How much courage to follow your innate intuition about the world do you have? How much pain of ignorance do you want to endure before facing yourself in the truth of present awareness? Here, you are infinitely loved by the universe of consciousness.

It is here, in your aware presence, that you will find your true identity based on consciousness.

Haven't we already established how awareness is our irrefutable, undeniable identity? Its characteristics and qualities are universal: love, acceptance, forgiveness, kindness, wisdom, spiritual intelligence, peace and above all, the sacred presence.

EVOLUTION OF AWARENESS

There are many mysteries in the world, such as ghosts, UFOs, aliens, the first cell's origin, evolution, prehistory, the rise of civilisations, pyramids, bigfoot, conspiracies, cancers, viruses, AI, Tunguska, the Moon, the Universe, existence, etc. But the all-time greatest mystery is the fact that we are aware, our capacity for self-awareness and consciousness. Even though most people are oblivious to their most basic nature, they are constantly perceiving it.

In the Western world, we identify consciousness with a waking state, next to dreaming and sleeping. So, for example, if you were hit on the head or felt weak and collapsed, you would be deemed as having lost consciousness, entering an unconscious state. Hence the term 'to be knocked unconscious.' But that is not the reality of the situation.

What really happens is that you lose your waking awareness, but consciousness is always fully present, always here as a fundamental background for experience and perception. So even when we lose our waking awareness, we can still experience dreaming or peaceful sleeping without dreaming. And even when our body dies, our awareness can still perceive and experience dimensions as a soul and spirit, as a God.

Every living being has its own point of awareness which is rooted in consciousness. Consciousness is the totality, one source of existence, the beingness.

By every being, I mean both animals and early humans, including modern tribes. We can call them primitive in a developmental sense, although we too fall behind more advanced alien beings, we can never disregard the fact that they have awareness. Again, perhaps we think they have undeveloped minds, perhaps they don't think in a way we are familiar with, with different reasoning and thought processes, but they are aware of their surroundings, and they are also sociable.

So we can not doubt their level of awareness, even an amoeba possesses the smallest sense of perception. And we could even go as far as calling some animals self-realised beings, again on the level of limited mental capacity, but with the ability to be silent and still, just as in the great apes.

We can even argue that we don't really have a civilisation, but more of an attempt at being civilised. Most of humanity suffers with a lack of basic human needs and are struggling to survive, so we are not civilised globally, and those who are, are being so at an enormous cost to human life and the environment.

Humans will never be entirely civilised, but a human can never be a complete beast or animal. To be human implies the use of tools and shelter; we must use tools to survive, which often leads to the development of large settlements that give rise to great civilisations.

In Native American lore, there is a being considered to be the perfect balance of natural, animalistic and human. They call him Sasquatch, while we call him Bigfoot and Yeti. This creature of legend is free like a wild animal but possesses enough self-awareness to be able to control itself. This view is, of course, hypothetical, as science still lacks a fossil or any living evidence of its existence, but the argument for its natural nature remains valid. Bigfoot, therefore, represents the perfect balance of nature and awareness. Animalistic enough not to require tools to survive, but conscious so that is not at the mercy of evolutionary biology. A supreme creature, the most perfect form of natural being.

At what point in the evolution of intelligence does awareness begin to recognise itself as consciousness?

Because great apes are already using tools, let's say they start using language and to live like early hominids and tribes did, at which point does their intelligence and awareness reach the highest point of unity?

We know the earliest Vedic poems and teachings date back to 3000 BC when they were passed down verbally until they were written in 1500 BC. So five thousand years ago humans had already reached the completion in consciousness that corresponds with the rise of the first great civilisations. Which begs the question, is the flowering of civilisation necessary for humans to reach the Zenit in consciousness?

Is a sufficient level of intelligence necessary for human self-realisation? Consciousness, of course, doesn't need an agent to be conscious, as it is already infinite and perfectly still. But an agent needs a certain level of intelligence to be able to delve into self-awareness and realise itself as consciousness.

The appearance of biological life and the evolution of self-awareness is truly the most remarkable phenomenon on the planet and anywhere else in the universe. It is the story of our present fascination, the journey to which we owe our capacity as conscious beings.

Humanity has, for the most part, forgotten that it is aware though. It is but a small investment into a necessary experience. Nothing in God's great plan of existence is bad or is not meant to be. All is a dance of energy, intention and awareness, the intensity of experience, the tranquillity of beingness.

Awareness can't be created or destroyed, but it is birthed through myriads of forms, all as a movement of consciousness. Like energy, it changes its shape but can't ever disappear. Awareness is a contraction of infinite consciousness into a finite self, in order to have experience. Knowing this, life is a dream of consciousness about a separate self via awareness, but it can be a beautiful and fulfilling dream.

Dreams only refer to something temporary. There is no such thing as not real. Everything experienced is real and it contributes to the opening of awareness towards pure consciousness. Life is a dream in the sense that it is temporary, so dreams have the same validity as life does, especially the lucid ones, if we learn from them.

The ability to be aware & still is the greatest blessing in existence, as it is self-evident existential magnificence.

If you were a rock, you obviously wouldn't be aware of existence, that is a privilege bestowed only upon biological creatures, however, all organic life likely experiences a certain degree of awareness as a base for their multitude of sense perceptions. But to be self-aware requires a more complex nervous system, such as in certain wildlife including elephants, dolphins and great apes. To be consciously aware is still exclusively a human trait.

Surely, we should explore the uniqueness that's within animal kingdom, making use of the fact that we are the only species of human to survive the evolutionary ages, (with possible genetic alterations from an outside party) and develop into a global society. This is a crucial time to become serious about our self-aware survival and take a more environmentally conscious way to securing life for the coming eons.

Our consciousness is the way.

Abiding as awareness is the most direct vestige into sacred presence, radiating with the light of the source itself. The great mystery of life and being is truly this straightforward and simple that it hides behind only a thought, dwelling in a lost moment and a mistaking of attention for fragments of ego's empowering trap.

But how do you keep feeding a non-existent phantom when its food is also an illusory belief in a false sense of identity, an entity that has been robbing us of the most holy dignity for countless centuries?

How do we even know we are aware? Take the moments before falling asleep for instance. You know you are present while laying there, but when you fall asleep you are not aware of that moment. It is only when you dream that you can be lucid, fully self-aware or even have something to remember. But without a dream, there is nothing consciousness can reflect upon, nothing to be aware of, so it doesn't remember anything, it rests in nothingness.

Self-awareness is self-evident. We can notice it in one's ability to remain still, in the absence of thought, and in the authentic wisdom shared in the moment. But the most obvious and appreciated, at least in the spiritual community, is the absence of ego.

That ability, that state of grace and wise kind-heartedness is the ultimate statement of the self-aware being. One recognises oneself as awareness and abides in a state of constant attention, awareness and pure beingness.

The only way you can know anything is if you are aware of it and you are aware of yourself. But notice that only awareness can be aware of anything, only awareness is aware, and only awareness can be aware of awareness.

By the definition of being aware, you are the awareness itself. You are aware, and you are awareness. By noticing even more fundamental truth, there is no you, there is only awareness, a stream of consciousness.

Awareness is, and awareness IS.
Awareness is as it is.
The presence is awareness.
Inseparable consciousness,
the present moment, the now.

Everybody is constantly aware, so we cannot stop the awareness, but we can focus it on different things and devote our attention to this or that. Most commonly, we direct our attention towards what we are looking at, doing, listening, thinking, feeling, hearing, sensing or perceiving in any way. All of this often happens involuntarily. It is almost as if we are trying to catch up with our awareness, as attention is running rampant all over the current experiences.

But how often are we aware of our attention or even of the awareness itself? How often are we aware of breathing or of the inner stillness that is residing as our peaceful being? How often are you not falling victim to unconscious urges and desires? How often are you in control of your attention? How often are you at one with your awareness?

If your response is mostly negative to these questions, then these questions beg to be asked: are you even alive and real, or more of a natural program, unconscious of yourself, unable to lead your life, like an animal with no control of its destiny and a victim of evolution?

Because if you are not aware, if you are not conscious or present, you can only be unaware, unconscious and not present. We must further ask what is the point of such an unconscious existence? What would be the purpose of existing but not knowing that you exist, at least not fully?

So you see, consciousness is the only legitimate foundation of being, without which there would be no knowing of experience, no awareness of being aware and no attention paid to the perceived.

*Being aware of being aware is, therefore, the holy mark
of sentience, the sacred presence as the awareness.*

We can further conclude how one's self-awareness
is the most important quality in existence, despite
not being crucial or necessary for survival.

Animals and vegetation are unconscious but evolution
has favoured their multiplication and growth, so much
that, together with geological elements, they are the
main components of what we consider to be nature.

If anything, self-awareness is doomed to extinction
sooner or later. And we can observe in the fossil record
that it is rather sooner than later. It takes a long time for
consciousness to be awakened in a biological being,
but it only takes moments for it to cease.

It is common knowledge how the more developed,
educated, intelligent and conscious individuals and
societies tend to have fewer offspring. And it is also well
known how fully self-realised beings create no offspring
at all, so it is logical to conclude how full consciousness
will mean the end of civilisation.

Civilisations seem to spring and blossom, as long
as they have enough unconsciousness to keep them
continuing to multiply. But, as civilisation enters a more
developed stage, the population begins to shrink and,

together with the natural changes and catastrophes,
it spells the end.

All this doesn't mean we should ignore our awareness.
Regardless of what the future holds, awareness is self-
evident and is part of the evolutionary process of
consciousness. We can indeed train ourselves to expand
our capacity for self-awareness, but often consciousness
is simply the awareness that happens without any effort
from the individual.

In that regard, awareness truly is a gift from God.
It is a sacred presence. But since we have become aware
of it, we have learned to practice and teach ourselves
to be more self-aware and more aware of awareness.

You and I, dear soul, have the same awareness at our
disposal. With it, we have the responsibility to protect
and cherish it, to educate future generations of their
capacity to be self-aware and of their ability to abide
in its conscious sacred presence.

PRACTICING AWARENESS

Knowing yourself as awareness is not something
someone can teach you. They can point to it, but only
you have your awareness to relate to and identify with.

Similarly, nobody can teach you how to be at peace in

nature, in your room or anywhere. You have your peace to be peaceful, you are already what you want to be, you just need to relax and realise it. You already are a human being with the fullest conscious capacity. We are only conditioned to think that there is something more extraordinary to life, so we tend to keep it complicated.

Real awakening is a return to the natural
simplicity of your awareness.

Before we were man or woman, beautiful or ugly, happy or sad, good or bad, rich or poor, taken or single, we just were. We were a pure presence of being. Such presence doesn't care for gender, social status or polarities of any kind.

Next time you feel agitated by something, stay with your awareness. Know from experience how this annoyance, reaction, provocation, hate, the need to defend and be right, is not you or your constant state. Feel how this surge of energy is merely a consequence of the present experience and how, beneath its triggered surface, there is a real you that is aware of the thoughts and emotional responses.

The real you as the awareness is deeply present, infinitely patient, kindly loving and wisely approachable.

This real you doesn't fight, argue, resist, blame or accuse. It doesn't confront, it comforts; it doesn't hurt, it heals. This sacred presence of your awareness cherishes every being with the familiar universal gesture of friendship recognised as the unwavering gaze of utmost acceptance, the common recognition of what makes us human, of what makes us alive, and of what portrays the transcendental soul values of being an aware welcoming being.

Awareness doesn't suddenly change its face, becoming hostile or offended. Awareness is the present power that pre-empts any disturbance in the body's energy field. But this doesn't happen by itself. You, as an aware being, need to align yourself with your awareness to benefit from such natural power of self-control. Any instance of failure to do so will inevitably lead to unconscious action/reaction patterns. So you will end up playing the role of a character that you believe you are, instead of knowing your aware presence and anticipating any unconscious traits of behaviour.

Being conscious of your breathing is the obvious way to enter the dimension of your aware space, allowing you to thus abide in the power of choice, to freely remain peaceful and ultimately access the direct knowledge of how to deal with any particular situation based on illuminated intuition.

Once again, the qualities of such wisdom are love, patience, the know-how, centred in the fearless certainty of being an eternal soul with nothing to lose, plus everything already gained in the moment-by-moment spiritual aspiration with the end reward of abiding in blissfulness.

Next time you feel lost in your reaction and drawn by the ego's need to protect itself, to be in control and to be right, regain the power of your aware presence. Stop, breathe and realise the eternal moment of the unchanging freshness of being safe and loving throughout any situation that arises only on the surface of an ocean of consciousness.

Next time, instead of engaging in fight or flight mode, simply disengage any ego's attempt at winning the argument. You will find a much bigger, more pleasant prize through abiding as awareness, as well as in sharing love, inspiration, peace and happiness with anyone who crosses your way.

By this intention of caring brilliance, you will surely overcome any unnecessary experience caused by the lack of awareness. For in complete attentiveness towards the now, we experience only the sacred presence of universal beingness. So be it.

Be grateful for the blessing of being aware. Give thanks and praise to God for giving you the miracle of being present and aware. In a world where so many suffer, you have been cherished and chosen by the universe to awaken the light of presence to those who are experiencing the darkness of unconsciousness. Be their support in times of need, for you know how much you have been grateful for help before when it was freely offered to you. You have been through it all, you know the value of selflessness, action, education and leading by being an example.

YOUR BEING IS GOD'S BEING

We have come a long way in human evolution to the point of transcending reality by coming back to experience raw reality – the present. After millennia of servitude to our ancient urges and modern mind involvements, now we are reclaiming the conscious presence by means of full self-awareness. We have truly reunited with God, as the sacred source of life.

Your natural presence is sacred because it is a self-evident quality of complete awareness, self-illuminating as the purest state of consciousness and a fully present perception unique in the natural world. For this reason, we don't have to believe it, we don't have to be faithful, for we are the love and fearlessness that we admire so much in saints, mystics and God.

God is the only natural state of existence.
We are all in God although we are thought to be separate.
We are one and the same consciousness that God is.
We are the oneness of being.

God is the feeling of appreciation for the blessing of being,
it is our living essence, one consciousness.

The peace, love, blessing and success we seek in
and from God, can, in truth, only be found in ourselves,
as the presence of our being. This, however, doesn't
mean we shouldn't interact with what we feel as God,
as long as it is beneficial for our well-being and if
it brings happiness to people around us.

Otherwise, it is an abusive relationship, which
can only mean it is not based on unconditional love
but on fear, manipulation and dogma.

Don't mistreat, abuse or dishonour God by making
him an outside object of neediness, calling on him only
in dire situations, forgetting him the rest of the time.

In contrast, don't make him an idol of worship,
don't be so obsessed and clingy towards him.
All humans desire to be loved, and God is the ultimate
excuse to feel loved by him, but rather awaken that
divine love within, the one that is not dependent
on circumstances, people or objects.

To that effect, you will not be dependent on God, as *she* is the love within you.

But society has taught us that we are physical creatures, almost unworthy of God's love. So how are we supposed to discover the love within us with such a low evolutionary opinion of ourselves? Isn't it more natural to feel worthy, healthy and capable of thinking and being with your own awareness, rather than being a fearful subject of a patriarchal hierarchy?

We all have the same, equal awareness, so nobody is better or worse than another. Sharing our inner wisdom merely reminds us of the common true self in everyone.

There is no big secret to life or awakening, we are all simply the consciousness, witnessing the miracle of existence. There are no minds, no individuals, no egos. There are only degrees of confusion within it or unconsciousness.

We can conclude that only awareness is real and permanent, while everything that we are aware of is illusory and temporary. Illusory doesn't necessarily imply unreal, but it points to its impermanent nature, compared to consciousness' infinity.

Notice how almost all of humanity's involvements are in temporary, illusory, and finite things and experiences.

We have invested everything into doing rather than
being. We cannot sit in peace for a few minutes without
doing something, be it engaging in conversation,
watching, listening, playing, working, addiction,
pleasure, eating, drinking, owning and so on.

Religions are trying to focus on spirituality,
but, again, most of it is based on worship.

And I tell you now that you don't need to do
anything to feel worthy or meaningful, to feel like you
belong or to feel powerful. Because simply being is
all that is necessary to be; we are beingness itself.

Then, finally, the breath is light, consciousness is alive
and present through one's awareness, through one's well
and joyful heart, in the gaze of each moment's blissfulness. The sun is burning inside, reflecting the soul's
permeating pleasantness. Its beingness washes you with
luminosity. Its warmth embraces your every cell with the
softest grace, a promise based on the certainty of being
aware, as you are the awareness – sacred and present.

We do this by becoming aware of our peaceful nature
that underlies all our experiences and perceptions. Be
that knowing of timelessness, the space in which existence appears, the consciousness that permeates all things.
Be open to the universal magnitude of things, emanating

right here as your shining awareness.

By knowing yourself as such present reality, you are looking straight from God's beingness.

All experiences and involvements shall pass,
all but that singular exposition of being aware.

I tell you: invest everything into your being, and you will know God as you know yourself by being aware of your being. There really is no other than that one self, expressing his familiarity with God by seeing him in every other being, the myriads of selves.

Such a heart of knowing is loving and kind. When freed from the mind, it fulfils what was prophesised by boundless consciousness. Its eternal vigil welcomes all who are ready to look beyond the phantom self and allow themselves to stay present, no matter the experience. You, too, can achieve its objective of unceasing blissfulness. You only need to melt the idea of a separate self from God's sacred presence, your imperishable awareness.

If we are lucky, we each have a few conscious decades of life on Earth, more or less, before the great unknown sends us back into the universe. That's a few aware decades to ponder and investigate the existential mystery. And you can force your way through, you can melt into the system or you can stand out from the crowd and truly allow your being to take on its natural inquisitor's role. You can stand in front of civilisation in a state of complete thoughtlessness and realise your truest self. You can jumpstart the long generational burden of fitting into the societal roles and thus become liberated to create new ways of being that fit in with current necessities as well as universal possibilities.

This is your duty as a conscious soul, dear human. This is your destiny as a realised universal being. This oath is to be your greatest blessing, that has so far been lying dormant. But now, instead of losing your authenticity to the familiar ways of working as part of the system, you have opened up your heart's secrets, you have woken up the sleeping giants of mental strength, and you have dared to see and venture into the expanded horizons of your soul's destiny on Earth.

I can but congratulate you for joining the higher cause of this sacred spiritual preservation that you will express through the open channels of your entire aware being, thus providing you with the present benefits that come with daring to be honest and conscious of your awareness.

I Love You as another you, as another me,
and as the oneness of we.

You are always welcome to abide in the grace
of our hearts, in the beauty of our souls and in
the cherished light of our aware being.

May we remain in this silent celebration of such
a loving being and the wise conscious presence,
as we have always meant to be.

Petar Umiljanović,

was born in Croatia on the 28th of June 1987.

From an early age, He felt strangely connected to and interested in the Universe, Nature, Religion, and Mysteries, along with Science, History, Ufology, Sport, and Music.

Later, profound insights into Psychology, Philosophy, and Spirituality led Him to investigate the True nature of the Self, revealing Consciousness as the only constant Presence.

Upon moving to Ireland and travelling Europe, thus engaging in many arts and activities, especially experiencing a deep relationship with Nature, this book was gradually inspired.

Contact:
petarumiljanovic@gmail.com

Notes

Notes